30 DAYS

TO A

NEW
BEGINNING

30 DAYS

TO A

NEW

BEGINNING

DAILY DEVOTIONS TO HELP YOU MOVE FORWARD

ABIDAN SHAH, PHD
& NICOLE SHAH

DEDICATION

This devotional is dedicated to our children:
Rebecca, Abigail, Nicholas, and Thomas.

"[We] have no greater joy than to hear that [our]
children walk in truth."   —3 John 4

CONTENTS

INTRODUCTION

After the success of *30 Days Through a Crisis*, we were asked when the next "30 Days" devotional would come out. To be honest, we hadn't planned on a sequel. We only wrote the first book to help people navigate their faith through the impacts of the pandemic, the political upheaval, and all the shutdowns of 2020. People needed hope and direction, and we were glad that God laid on our hearts to write that book. Since its publication, we have heard from so many people about how much that book meant to them. We give God the glory.

This book has a different emphasis. The year 2022 has been a year of new beginnings in our family. In January, our daughter Abigail married her sweetheart, Jarrett; in May, our son Nicholas graduated from high school and started college; in September, our daughter Rebecca married her love, Ed; and in October, our youngest son Thomas got his driver's license.

To write a book on new beginnings was both overwhelming and satisfying. New beginnings can be tough for both the lead character and the supporting cast. As each of our children moved forward in the journey God had for them, we also had to discover and embrace our new roles. This is never easy, but by God's grace we have been able to revel and grow in this season of new beginnings.

Once again, thanks are due to the Clearview team. John Galantis served as the editor of this project. His ability to help us draw out what we were trying to communicate and make it impactful was truly impressive. Also, the weekly "pep texts" were motivating and hilarious! Ryan Hill helped with the editing and creating of the design and layout. He did it again! Thanks to Kelsey McKeel for reading the chapters and making helpful comments. David Williamson not only helped with the book, but he also assists me (Abidan) with all my teaching responsibilities and other obligations—and he does all of it with joy and willingness. We also thank each of their family and loved ones. Any faults with the book are our responsibility.

We are especially grateful to our Clearview Church family and our leadership. It is such a joy to know that we are surrounded and supported by people who exemplify the chapters of this book.

May this book guide you in the new beginning that God has for you. As you move forward, our prayer is that you will move closer to Christ through his Word and in the power of the Holy Spirit. After all, that is the true goal of life.

1. FEELING STUCK

Human beings are prone to getting stuck in a rut.

It's inevitable—no matter how well-organized we are, no matter how far ahead we plan, we all fall into a rut at some point. A rut of complacency, inaction, and—dare we say it—fear keeps us paralyzed. There's an old saying: "The only difference between a rut and the grave is the depth." Isn't that the truth? Still...why does this happen? Are we afraid of facing the challenges ahead of us? Do we simply grow comfortable in our misery?

Whatever the reason, one thing is certain—when we fail to move forward in life, we miss out on the blessings that God has in store for us. And how do we respond? We blame others or wallow in self-pity! After all, doesn't that feel better than accepting responsibility for our own inaction? It's much easier to complain and compare than to confront our complacency.

This is nothing new. The people of Israel were stuck for forty years in the wilderness. They were at Mount Sinai for eleven months encountering God, receiving the gift of the Law, seeing the holiness of God, and building the Tabernacle...and none of this was a waste of time. But, instead of moving forward with renewed faith, they decided to camp there indefinitely. God had to push them out!

As they made their way to Kadesh Barnea, God used Moses to organize them. They had witnessed enough wonders to know that God was with them. They could see the Promised Land laid out right before them, but, yet again, instead of moving forward in faith, they refused God's command to take the land for themselves. As a result, God condemned that generation to die in the wilderness over the next thirty-eight years. Only Moses, Joshua, and Caleb survived because they alone believed God and were willing to move forward in obedience.

You'd think this would be enough to warn the next generation—nope! They too decided to hesitate and skirt Mount Seir! God had to tell them what he had told their parents and grandparents at Mount Sinai forty years earlier: "Enough going in circles! Move forward!"

Here are some questions for you to consider: Are you stuck in a rut? Are you wasting time going in circles? If so, what's keeping you from moving forward? Would you rather skirt that mountain in your life than step out in faith? Do you blame others for your indecisions? Is crying and complaining easier than climbing and conquering? These are tough questions but unless you answer them honestly, there can be no progress in your life.

The place to begin is not self-determination, an iron will, or even clarifying your goals or strategies. Begin by clarifying who God is and what that means for your life. People who serve a big God attempt big things for him. More often than not, our lack of movement is directly proportional to the size of our God.

But it's not enough to simply believe in a big God. You also have to know his heart for you. The only way to come to him is by first coming to his Son, Jesus Christ. Jesus said, "I am the way, the truth, and the life. No one comes to the Father except through me" (John 14:6). If you don't know Jesus, receive him today as your savior and king. If you do know him, it's time to get unstuck from the rut and move forward!

Scriptures to Think On:

The Lord our God spoke to us in Horeb, saying: "You have dwelt long enough at this mountain. Turn and take your journey…" **Deuteronomy 1:6-7a**

…and we skirted Mount Seir for many days. And the Lord spoke to me, saying: "You have skirted this mountain long enough; turn northward…" **Deuteronomy 2:1-3**

Have I not commanded you? Be strong and of good courage; do not be afraid, nor be dismayed, for the Lord your God is with you wherever you go. **Joshua 1:9**

"...and lo, I am with you always, even to the end of the age." Amen. **Matthew 28:20c**

JOURNAL

_____

_____

_____

_____

_____

_____

_____

_____

_____

_____

_____

_____

2. PRAYER

Imagine for a moment that you were given a special "goal" phone. You can use this phone anytime you need, as long as it's to help you move forward and reach your goal. It doesn't matter if your need is physical, emotional, spiritual, financial, relational, informational, or directional… all you have to do is dial the number, and there is someone on the other side, twenty-four hours a day, ready, able, and more than willing to help you out!

Too good to be true, right?

Well, that's what prayer is! Not only does it work, but it is indispensable if you are to move forward and reach your goal. Scripture is replete with examples of men and women praying to God when they needed something to reach their goals:

- Abraham prayed for a child. God answered him in due time. (Genesis 21:2)
- Jacob asked God for protection from his brother Esau. The preincarnate Christ came down himself to break him but make him stronger in his weakness. (Genesis 32:30)
- Moses prayed to God for direction to lead the people of Israel. God promised him his

presence and his rest. (Exodus 33:14)

- Hannah prayed to God in much anguish and weeping for a child. He answered her prayer and gave her the greatest judge and leader that Israel ever knew. (1 Samuel 1:20)
- Solomon prayed for wisdom to lead God's people. God answered him with wisdom, riches beyond imagination, and honor as the last king of the unified kingdom. (1 Kings 2:13)
- Esther asked all the Jewish people in Shushan to fast (which involved prayers) along with her as she went before the king to intercede for them. God saved them from annihilation. (Esther 4:16)
- Jonah prayed to God from inside the big fish. God spoke to the fish and it vomited Jonah on dry land. (Jonah 2:10)
- Jesus prayed to his father throughout his earthly ministry (Matthew 14:23) and especially on the night when he was betrayed. God the Father answered by sending an angel to strengthen him. (Luke 22:43)
- On the day of Pentecost, as the disciples were gathered in prayer, the Holy Spirit came upon them in all power, and the church was born. (Acts 2)
- The ministry of Peter, Paul, and the New Testament church was marked by constant prayers, and God answered in amazing ways.

As you're making your way to a new beginning in life, begin each day with prayer. Thank God for all the blessings in your life—and be specific! Next, pray for the people who are close to you. If you know about specific issues that they're struggling with, pray over those. Then finally, pray for yourself. Pray that God would change you and mold you into the person that he's created you to be.

If praying is hard for you (or something new and unfamiliar), pretend that Jesus is sitting in the room with you, and you are having a conversation with him. All he wants you to do is talk to him and ask for whatever you need in childlike faith. His word is true. He will answer your prayers according to his will and purpose in your life. He will help you move forward and reach your goal.

Scriptures to Think On:

And Jabez called on the God of Israel saying, "Oh, that You would bless me indeed, and enlarge my territory, that Your hand would be with me, and that You would keep me from evil, that I may not cause pain!" So God granted him what he requested.   **1 Chronicles 4:10**

The Lord is near to all who call upon him, to all who call upon him in truth.   **Psalm 145:18**

Then you will call upon Me and go and pray to Me, and I will listen to you.   **Jeremiah 29:12**

In this manner, therefore, pray: "Our Father in heaven, hallowed be Your name. Your kingdom come. Your will be done on earth as it is in heaven. Give us this day our daily bread. And forgive us our debts, as we forgive our debtors. And do not lead us into temptation, but deliver us from the evil one. For Yours is the kingdom and the power and the glory forever. Amen." **Matthew 6:9-13**

Be anxious for nothing, but in everything by prayer and supplication, with thanksgiving, let your requests be made known to God; and the peace of God, which surpasses all understanding, will guard your hearts and minds through Christ Jesus.   **Philippians 4:6-7**

JOURNAL

_____

_____

_____

_____

_____

_____

_____

_____

_____

_____

_____

_____

_____

_____

_____

_____

_____

_____

3. MEDITATE ON GOD'S WORD

Any time our family goes on vacation or travels to a new place, we always make sure to get the best and latest travel guide. It may be old-school, but we still appreciate that a good travel guide has up-to-date maps with the clearest directions, answers to all the questions regarding the necessary requirements of your visit (visas or inoculation) and gives you a list of the best hotels and restaurants around. Of course, we also appreciate that they always have detailed descriptions of the various sites with their historical information, entry fees, and times. Finally, there are suggested itineraries based on days and finances.

We love being well-prepared and aware of all the necessaries.

Some people fly by the seat of their pants and figure things out along the way as they travel, but that's so risky. There's always some gem tucked away somewhere that people miss. So also, the Bible is God's travel guide for us in the journey of life. It gives us all the information we need to reach our destination. Unlike the spontaneous and extempore adventurers, you cannot afford to travel in life without the guidance of God's Word.

After Moses' death, God told Joshua to be make certain that, "This Book of the Law shall not depart from your mouth, but you shall meditate in it day and night, that you may observe to do according to all that is written in it. For then you will make your way prosperous, and then you will have good success" (Joshua 1:8).

Simply put, for Joshua to navigate through the Promised Land, find victory in battles, and help the entire nation of Israel settle successfully, it would require a daily reading of the Word of God. The key word in that command is "meditate." In Hebrew, the word is *hagah* which the *New International Dictionary of Old Testament Theology and Exegesis* defines as "deep, reflective thought, often occurring in a repetitive or enduring fashion."

It's not enough to just occasionally glance at the travel guide. You must read it carefully and commit it to memory if you truly want to benefit from the journey and reach the destination safely. The same is true with the Bible. You have to reflect on it! Start small—if you're ever reading the Bible and a verse seems to jump off the page at you, recognize that that's God speaking to you about something! Write that verse down, then write down how you can apply it to your life. Spend some time thinking and reflecting on that verse as you go about your day. Recite it and commit it to memory. Read it again before you go to sleep.

No matter what the world tells you, the Bible is extremely relevant to your life today. It tells of the people of God who were fallen—just like us—and how God moved in them and through them to fulfill his purpose for their lives. If you want to know what God is like, read the Bible. If you want to know what God's will is for your life, read the Bible. If you're struggling to see where he's taking you on your journey, read the Bible. If I could extend our original analogy, doing your daily devotions and meditating on God's Word is more than just reading the travel guide. It's also putting gas in the tank of your car. Reading the Bible not only tells you where to go, but it enables you to get there as well.

Scriptures to Think On:

Blessed is the man who walks not in the counsel of the ungodly, nor stands in the path of sinners, nor sits in the seat of the scornful; but his delight is in the law of the Lord, and in his law he meditates day and night. **Psalm 1:1-2**

I will meditate on Your precepts, and contemplate Your ways…Princes also sit and speak against me, but Your servant meditates on Your statutes…My eyes are awake through the night watches, that I may meditate on Your word. **Psalm 119: 15, 23, 148**

All Scripture is given by inspiration of God, and is profitable for doctrine, for reproof, for correction, for instruction in righteousness, that the man of God may be complete, thoroughly equipped for every good work. **2 Timothy 3:16-17**

For the word of God is living and powerful, and sharper than any two-edged sword, piercing even to the division of soul and spirit, and of joints and marrow, and is a discerner of the thoughts and intents of the heart. And there is no creature hidden from his sight, but all things are naked and open to the eyes of him to whom we must give account. **Hebrews 4:12-13**

JOURNAL

_____

_____

_____

_____

_____

_____

_____

_____

_____

_____

_____

_____

_____

_____

_____

_____

_____

_____

4. MOTIVATION

Motivation is the fuel that keeps us going in our journey. No matter where you're headed in life or how far you've come, motivation is critical to reaching your destination. Some of the most gifted and talented individuals give up in the face of obstacles because their motivation supply is low. Strangely enough, the averagely gifted and moderately talented individuals make it to the top. Their secret? Motivation.

I'll admit that I (Nicole) am not self-motivated at all. An outside source must motivate me to get out of bed in the morning, to start working out, even to further my education (Abidan has been the motivating force behind that one). It always starts blurry, but once I start to see the goal more clearly, motivation sets in and I find myself coming up with ideas of how to accomplish that goal. In our marriage, Abidan is the visionary, and I'm the one who sees the day-to-day. It works for us.

When Moses was certain his time had come, on God's command, he passed the baton to his successor, Joshua, with the following words: "Be strong and of good courage, for you must go with this people to the land which the Lord has sworn to their fathers to give them, and you shall cause them to inherit it. And the Lord, he is the one who goes before you. He will be with you. He will not leave you nor forsake you; do not fear nor be dismayed" (Deuteronomy 31:7-8). That phrase – "Be strong and of good courage" – is used repeatedly to motivate Joshua to lead the people into the Promised Land. God used Moses' encouragement to motivate Joshua to press forward.

I also can't help but think of Jesus in the Garden of Gethsemane. He asked his inner circle (Peter, James, and John) to stay awake with him and pray, but they failed. As the hour was drawing near for him to go to the cross, he knelt and prayed: "'Father, if it is your will, take this cup away from me; nevertheless not my will, but yours, be done.' At that very moment, an angel appeared to him from heaven to strengthen him" (Luke 22:42-43). In other words, God the Father sent an angel to his Son to motivate him to stay strong and press forward in his task.

How wonderful it is when we have the right people around to motivate us in our relationship goals, financial goals, health goals, spiritual goals, etc. However, there will be times when there is no one around to motivate you. There will also be times when people in your life actively work to demotivate and demoralize you. When you find yourself in those moments, follow King David's example: "But David strengthened himself in the Lord his God" (1 Samuel 30:6d).

Scriptures to Think On:

Unless the Lord had been my help, my soul would soon have settled in silence. If I say, "My foot slips," Your mercy, O Lord, will hold me up. **Psalm 94:17-18**

Therefore we also, since we are surrounded by so great a cloud of witnesses, let us lay aside every weight, and the sin which so easily ensnares us, and let us run with endurance the race that is set before us, looking unto Jesus, the author and finisher of our faith, who for the joy that was set before Him endured the cross, despising the shame, and has sat down at the right hand of the throne of God.   **Hebrews 12:1-2**

JOURNAL

_____

_____

_____

_____

_____

_____

_____

_____

_____

_____

_____

_____

_____

_____

_____

_____

_____

_____

5. RECAST THE PAST

History is a great teacher. It gives us insight, opportunities to learn from past mistakes, and clarity— not only for where things went wrong, but also for how we can improve. Yet for some reason, people often consider their past insignificant or worthless. From the rearview mirror, their story is nothing but a series of futile experiences with no tangible benefits. They fail to see any value in their failed endeavors, bad memories, and even traumatic moments.

In other words, their past is a painful reminder of how things never worked and never will.

The truth is, every part of our past has something positive to add to our present and our future! It's a matter of how we choose to look back.

Take Joseph for example: he was sold into slavery by his own brothers! Imagine how traumatic that must have been, how easy it would have been to resign himself to a life of self-pity and defeat. Yet, in spite of his past, Joseph chose to excel in his work. When Potiphar's wife falsely accused him and had him arrested, he excelled even in prison and was made in charge of the other inmates. In God's timing, Pharaoh had a dream with no one to interpret. When Joseph interpreted the dream, he was made second-in-command in Egypt and saved the people from a seven-year famine. Joseph's willingness to learn from his past and his refusal to be bitter brought such blessing to his life!

Even someone with a sinful past can be used by God for building his kingdom. Just think about the Samaritan woman in the book of John. Not only did the Samaritans falsely claim to be God's chosen ones (2 Kings 17), they also harassed the Jewish people after they returned from exile. Despite this tension, Jesus made a point to meet this woman on his journey from Judea to Galilee. During the conversation at the well, she tried to get into a theological debate with Jesus, but he saw through her and called her out on her adulterous lifestyle. She could have gotten defensive or angry. Instead, her eyes were opened, and she ran back to her city and told the people, "Come, see a man who told me all things that I ever did. Could this be the Christ?" (John 4:29).

As a result, many in the city were saved, and the doors were flung open for the Samaritans to come into the kingdom of God! This woman of ill-repute didn't bother trying to hide her dirty reputation from Jesus or from her city. She claimed ownership of her sin, and God used her past to capture hearts for the sake of the gospel. How beautiful is God's mercy!

The point is this: you are not limited by your past, whether you are the victim or the villain. We all make choices each day. I remember Nicole's father used to tell her all the time, "You have a choice. You can let life make you bitter...or you can let it make you better."

Examine your own past. Are you going to let it paralyze you? Or will you trust God and let him use your past to propel you forward?

Scriptures to Think On:

Only take heed to yourself, and diligently keep yourself, lest you forget the things your eyes have seen, and lest they depart from your heart all the days of your life. And teach them to your children and your grandchildren. **Deuteronomy 4:9**

Do not remember the former things, nor consider the things of old. Behold, I will do a new thing, now it shall spring forth; Shall you not know it? I will even make a road in the wilderness and rivers in the desert.
Isaiah 43:18-19

But Jesus said to him, "No one, having put his hand to the plow, and looking back, is fit for the kingdom of God." **Luke 9:62**

And we know that all things work together for good to those who love God, to those who are the called according to his purpose. **Romans 8:28**

JOURNAL

_____

_____

_____

_____

_____

_____

_____

_____

_____

_____

_____

_____

_____

_____

_____

_____

_____

6. UNREALISTIC EXPECTATIONS

Developing expectations is a healthy way to achieve your goal, but they have to be achievable. Unrealistic expectations are rigid, immovable things that serve only to kill your vision, obliterate your hopes and dreams, and taint your health and relationships—with people and with God!

After forty years of wandering through the wilderness, Moses brought the people of Israel to the borders of the Promised Land once again. Among many admonitions and reiterations, he reminded them: "You shall surely set a king over you whom the Lord your God chooses" (Genesis 17:15). Then, he gave them a list of qualifications for the king whom God approved.

Unfortunately, when Samuel came on the scene centuries later, the people disregarded Moses' list and demanded a king saying, "No, but we will have a king over us, that we also may be like all the nations..." (1 Samuel 8:19-20). Samuel was extremely upset with the people, but God told him to "Heed their voice, and make them a king" (1 Samuel 8:22).

As you know, Saul became that first king of Israel— hardly God's choice. In fact, when Samuel first encountered Saul, he was wandering around looking for his father's donkeys, an indication of his lack of wisdom and discernment. From day one, Saul made decisions that were impulsive and self-serving. He attacked his enemies unprovoked, offered unlawful sacrifices, insulted his mentor, and even failed to provide weapons to his own troops.

But perhaps the worst offense came when he laid an unrealistic expectation on his soldiers: "And the men of Israel were distressed that day, for Saul had placed the people under oath, saying, 'Cursed is the man who eats any food until evening, before I have taken vengeance on my enemies.' So none of the people tasted food. Now all the people of the land came to a forest; and there was honey on the ground. And when the people had come into the woods, there was the honey, dripping; but no one put his hand to his mouth, for the people feared the oath" (1 Samuel 14:24-26).

Can you imagine the distress these men were in? Ironically, Saul's own son Jonathan, unaware of his father's demands, ate some of the honey. "When Saul was informed, he proceeded to carry out the sentence of death on his own son. But the people said to Saul, 'Shall Jonathan die, who has accomplished this great deliverance in Israel? Certainly not! As the Lord lives, not one hair of his head shall fall to the ground, for he has worked with God this day.' So the people rescued Jonathan, and he did not die" (1 Samuel 14:45). Imagine having to be rescued from death due to the unrealistic expectations of your own father!

So, how can you tell when your expectations are unrealistic? The responses of the people around you are very good indicators. When you lay out your expectations for someone, pay attention to how they react. If they don't react well, you've most likely established unrealistic expectations on that person, expectations they knew that they couldn't meet.

We can also develop unrealistic expectations when it comes to God. When we pray for something specific and don't get what we prayed for, we can become disappointed or even angry with God. To combat unrealistic expectations with God, let your attitude be, "Your will, not mine." This is much easier said than done. It takes a daily laying down of your own desires, an unyielding trust in God's promises, and an expectation that God will do exactly what he says he will do.

Scripture to Think On:

My soul, wait silently for God alone, For my expectation is from him.   **Psalm 62:5**

The hope of the righteous will be gladness, But the expectation of the wicked will perish.   **Proverbs 10:28**

Fathers, do not provoke your children, lest they become discouraged.   **Colossians 3:21**

JOURNAL

_____

_____

_____

_____

_____

_____

_____

_____

_____

_____

_____

_____

_____

_____

_____

_____

_____

_____

7. PRIORITIZE

Whatever we prioritize gets done—period.

Too many times, people try to accomplish their goals without taking the time to prioritize them. They continue their normal habits, go about their normal schedule, and simply assume that their vision will somehow come to pass. They buy fancy gadgets and sign up for expensive programs as if throwing money at their goal will make up for their failure to prioritize.

Setting goals requires making changes to your daily routine. Those changes give you adequate time and necessary motivation to reach what you desire. An example comes to mind from the book of Nehemiah in the Old Testament.

Nehemiah left his high position in Persia and travelled to his ancestral homeland to help his people. Nebuchadnezzar, king of Babylon, had completely obliterated the city of Jerusalem, the Temple, and the city walls in 587 BC. Fifty years later, as promised, God brought his people back from exile and commanded them to rebuild everything. They finished the Temple by 516 BC, but the city walls still lay in ruins one hundred years later. There were many reasons for that – lack of leadership, motivation, unity, and the added pressure of opposition from their neighbors. The result was that there was no security, no stability, hopelessness, apathy, and worst of all, a loss of identity.

By much prayer, Nehemiah rallied the people to begin the work...but it wasn't easy. In the face of incredible opposition, little skill, and few resources, they finished the wall in only fifty-two days—a miraculous feat! A major reason for that was, as Nehemiah 4:6 says, "the people had a mind to work." In other words, under Nehemiah's leadership, the people not only made it a priority to rebuild the walls of Jerusalem, but they had an incredible drive to finish it, even in the face of direct opposition.

Do you have a mind to work? Have you taken the time to prioritize your goal? Try this: for one week, keep track of how you spend your time every day. Write down everything, even the time it takes you to get ready in the morning. Once you've done that, study it and take note of what takes up the most time. If you're noticing that you are running out of time every day to get everything done, consider restructuring your schedule so that the most important things get done first. Save the nonessentials for the end of the day.

Are your priorities in the right order? If not, rearrange them in the way that God is leading you to accomplish your goal. Here's a suggested list of properly ordered priorities: God should always be first in your life. That means spending time reading your Bible and praying. If you're married, your spouse comes next, followed by your children. After all, they were there before there were children and will hopefully be there once the kids are grown and have moved out. You need to foster that relationship. After your family comes your church family, then finally your job.

Your list may differ here and there, but the truth is this: in order to have a fresh start, you can't keep living the way you were. There must be an intentional shift in your priorities.

<u>Scriptures to Think On:</u>

Now set your heart and your soul to seek the Lord your God. Therefore arise and build the sanctuary of the Lord God, to bring the ark of the covenant of the Lord and the holy articles of God into the house that is to be built for the name of the Lord.   **2 Chronicles 22:19**

But seek first the kingdom of God and his righteousness, and all these things shall be added to you.   **Matthew 6:33**

…he is a double-minded man, unstable in all his ways. **James 1:8**

JOURNAL

8. BEWARE SHORTCUTS

Shortcuts can save you time, money, and effort, but they can also cause you to get disqualified.

Shortcuts aren't inherently wrong. When you're familiar with an area, you can avoid the main roads during rush hour and save time (or a potential fender bender). If you're technologically savvy, you can use some of your phone's advanced functions to save two or three unnecessary steps.

When it comes to life, however, shortcuts that involve taking something that increases performance or enables you to get results without having to put in effort are never healthy and may disqualify you. This applies to relationships, finances, sports, and even spiritual growth.

Right after his baptism, Jesus was led by the Holy Spirit into the wilderness where the devil tempted him with three shortcuts. Keep in mind, Satan is the master of shortcuts. In fact, the same shortcuts he offered to Jesus he had already offered to Adam and Eve, who fell for them and became disqualified, leading the whole human race to be disqualified along with them. But Jesus, the second Adam, would reject these shortcuts, qualifying himself to be our Savior.

Take a look at the first shortcut in Luke 4:3—"If You are the Son of God, command this stone to become bread." The first thing the devil tried was appeal to Jesus' appetite. Remember, he did the same thing to Eve in the Garden of Eden when he convinced her that the tree was good for food (Genesis 3:6).

The second shortcut is in Luke 4:5-7—"Then the devil, taking him up on a high mountain, showed him all the kingdoms of the world in a moment of time. And the devil said to him, 'All this authority I will give You, and their glory; for this has been delivered to me, and I give it to whomever I wish. Therefore, if You will worship before me, all will be Yours.'" This time, Satan appealed to Jesus' eyes, much like he tempted Eve in Genesis 3:6 who thought the fruit was "pleasant to the eyes."

What's the final shortcut? Take a look at Luke 4:9-11—"Then he brought him to Jerusalem, set him on the pinnacle of the temple, and said to him, 'If You are the Son of God, throw Yourself down from here. For it is written: "He shall give his angels charge over you, to keep you," and, "In their hands they shall bear you up, Lest you dash your foot against a stone."'" Satan tried to appeal to Jesus' pride! Once again, remember Eve who saw that it was "a tree desirable to make one wise" (Genesis 3:6).

Never forget that Satan's shortcuts—appetite, pleasure, and pride—haven't changed, albeit they come in different packages. As 1 John 2:16 warns, "For all that is in the world—the lust of the flesh, the lust of the eyes, and the pride of life—is not of the Father but is of the world."

How did Jesus respond to these shortcuts? He quoted Deuteronomy against each one. Luke 4:4-12 says, "Man shall not live by bread alone, but by every word of God," and "You shall worship the Lord your God, and him only you shall serve," and finally, "You shall not tempt the Lord your God."

As you're tempted by shortcuts, always respond with the truth of Scripture. Remember, Adam and Eve took the devil's shortcuts and damned us all into sin, but Jesus took the long road and delivered us unto salvation!

Scriptures to Think On:

Treasures of wickedness profit nothing, but righteousness delivers from death.   **Proverbs 10:2**

There is a way that seems right to a man, but its end is the way of death.   **Proverbs 14:2**

Enter by the narrow gate; for wide is the gate and broad is the way that leads to destruction, and there are many who go in by it. Because narrow is the gate and difficult is the way which leads to life, and there are few who find it.   **Matthew 7:13-14**

For in that he himself has suffered, being tempted, he is able to aid those who are tempted.   **Hebrews 2:18**

JOURNAL

_____

_____

_____

_____

_____

_____

_____

_____

_____

_____

_____

_____

_____

_____

_____

_____

_____

9. EMOTIONS

Emotions can function as natural turbo boosters when pressing towards your goal. They can give you the afterburner to thrust forward when you feel like giving up, or they can serve as a pressure release valve when everything feels too overwhelming to carry on.

Unfortunately, emotions can also be at the root of countless problems. They can cause you to lose your sense of discernment and even quit before you reach the finish line. A biblical understanding of emotions can help you use them to your advantage.

To begin with, God created your emotions. In fact, he himself has emotions! The Bible tells us that God experiences satisfaction, compassion, delight, and anger just to name a few. Jesus demonstrated a range of emotions during his earthly ministry, from joy and satisfaction to anger and sadness. Moreover, since God has made us in his image, we have been created to have emotions. In other words, emotions are not evil; they are God's gift to us to enjoy him, his world, and the life he has given us.

We can all agree that Simon Peter was an emotional man. In the middle of a storm on the Sea of Galilee, he sees Jesus walking on the waves and begs to join him. Then, he sees the boisterous wind and starts doubting, causing him to sink.

And when Jesus asks his disciples in Matthew 16, "Who do men say that I, the Son of Man, am?" only Peter gives the correct answer: "You are the Christ, the Son of the living God." Jesus commends him, but in the very next passage, Peter scolds Jesus for talking about his imminent crucifixion and resurrection. Here, we encounter Jesus' infamous rebuke of Peter – "Get behind Me, Satan!" Similar incidents occur when Peter decides to follow Jesus on the night of the crucifixion, even though he was warned not to do so. He even denied Jesus three times!

Nonetheless, it was also Peter's fearless faith that qualified him to preach that powerful message on the Day of Pentecost. Later, he was also instrumental in opening the door to the Gentiles with the pouring out of the Holy Spirit in the house of Cornelius.

Properly used, emotions can be marvelous. Misused, they can be disastrous. In other words, let your emotions give you the extra boost or the safety valve you need, but don't make them the foundation of your goal. God made us emotional beings, but he never intended for us to be ruled by our feelings. If we are constantly being swayed by our emotions, we will never stick with anything. To keep moving forward despite our feelings takes God's power and our discipline. As J. Sidlow Baxter would say, "Your emotions are the shallowest part of your nature. God doesn't do his deepest work in the shallowest part."

Scriptures to Think On:

A merry heart does good, like medicine, but a broken spirit dries the bones. **Proverbs 17:22**

Whoever has no rule over his own spirit is like a city broken down, without walls.   **Proverbs 25:28**

These things I have spoken to you, that My joy may remain in you, and that your joy may be full.
John 15:11

Now may the God of hope fill you with all joy and peace in believing, that you may abound in hope by the power of the Holy Spirit.   **Romans 15:13**

JOURNAL

_____

_____

_____

_____

_____

_____

_____

_____

_____

_____

_____

_____

_____

_____

_____

_____

_____

_____

10. BUILD GOOD HABITS

Contrary to popular belief, it actually takes longer than three weeks to create a habit. According to Phillippa Lally, a health psychology researcher from University College in London, it can take anywhere between sixty-six and two-hundred fifty-four days to fully develop a powerful habit. This means you must be determined if you want to build habits that will keep you on the path to a fresh start. It means you must decide on actions that will keep you on a forward trajectory in life, then stick to those decisions!

Of course, there will be times when you'll fall off the wagon. But that doesn't mean you should stop or give up on your habit-building. You just pick up where you left off and keep going!

Although the word "habit" is never found in Scripture, there are synonyms that illustrate the same concept. One example we find in both the Old and New Testaments is the word "training," especially with regards to rearing children in the right way. "Train up a child in the way he should go, and when he is old, he will not depart from it" (Proverbs 22:6). God gave special instructions to Israel in order to train their children diligently in his words. And what was his key instruction? Start young!

"And these words which I command you today

shall be in your heart. You shall teach them diligently to your children, and shall talk of them when you sit in your house, when you walk by the way, when you lie down, and when you rise up. You shall bind them as a sign on your hand, and they shall be as frontlets between your eyes. You shall write them on the doorposts of your house and on your gates" (Deuteronomy 6:6).

In other words, make it a habit to discuss God's word with your children. Don't just teach them with words; model it for them! Paul underscores this command in his letter to the Ephesians: "bring them up in the training and admonition of the Lord" (Ephesians 6:4).

Jesus reiterated the idea of habit-building in the teacher-disciple relationship: "A disciple is not above his teacher, but everyone who is perfectly trained will be like his teacher" (Luke 6:40).

Just as God wants us to train our children to develop good habits early in life, so also, we must create good habits for ourselves, habits that help us accomplish our goal—and do it sooner rather than later. Developing good habits will strengthen you on days when you don't feel like pressing on or you feel overwhelmed by life. Even Jesus had two helpful habits—albeit different words are utilized. "And as his custom was, he went into the synagogue on the Sabbath day" (Luke 4:16), and "So he himself often withdrew into the wilderness and prayed" (Luke 5:16). Attending the synagogue weekly and praying alone daily were the habits of the Son of God. Perhaps we should take a page from his book and do the same!

Take a moment to reflect: What are your healthy habits? Do you have any that you're already implementing? If not, what small action can you take right now? And are you willing to commit to that action for a week? A month? Three months? Don't be content with simply daydreaming about how you're going to change. Begin now. You'll be glad you did later.

Scriptures to Think On:

Some Gadites joined David at the stronghold in the wilderness, mighty men of valor, men trained for battle, who could handle shield and spear, whose faces were like the faces of lions, and were as swift as gazelles on the mountains. **1 Chronicles 12:8**

Blessed be the Lord my Rock, who trains my hands for war, and my fingers for battle. **Psalm 144:1**

Now no chastening seems to be joyful for the present, but painful; nevertheless, afterward it yields the peaceable fruit of righteousness to those who have been trained by it. **Hebrews 12:11**

JOURNAL

_____

_____

_____

_____

_____

_____

_____

_____

_____

_____

_____

_____

_____

_____

_____

_____

_____

_____

_____

11. GAMEPLAN

A vision without a gameplan is just a daydream. Most people daydream about their marriage, children, career, education, or retirement— but they don't have a plan of how they are going to actually accomplish those things. Unfortunately, those dreams never materialize.

The Bible has several instances in which people used gameplans to achieve their vision. One of my favorites is when Abraham sent his servant Eliezer to find a wife for his son, Isaac. Abraham didn't want Isaac to marry a Canaanite woman, because the Canaanites didn't walk in the way of God, nor did they understand the coming of God's salvation through Abraham's descendants.

Eliezer was Abraham's most trusted and mature servant. When he arrived in Nahor, where Abraham's family dwelt, he did not immediately launch into the task of locating a bride. Instead, he prayed to God very specifically: "Behold, here I stand by the well of water, and the daughters of the men of the city are coming out to draw water. Now let it be that the young woman to whom I say, 'Please let down your pitcher that I may drink,' and she says, 'Drink, and I will also give your camels a drink'—let her be the one you have appointed for your servant Isaac" (Genesis 24:12-14).

Even before he could finish praying, Rebekah arrived with a pitcher on her shoulder, and she did everything according to Eliezer's prayer. Eliezer maturely restrained his excitement, asking for her family connections and if there was room for him, his men, and the camels to lodge.

On meeting Rebekah's brother, Laban, who showed hospitality by laying food before him, Eliezer refused to eat until he gave the reason for his visit. After explaining his strategy and the answer of God in sending Rebekah, Eliezer asked if the proposal was accepted. When given the affirmation, he praised God and gave gifts to Rebekah and her family. The next morning, he declined Laban's offer to remain ten days there and insisted on taking Rebekah back that very day. Rebekah agreed and went with Eliezer to marry Isaac.

Eliezer's strategy is a wonderful example of building a gameplan on convictions, maturity, prayer, precise expectations, gifts to please others, and not deviating from the purpose of the journey.

God is sovereign, but he won't just hand things over to you. He wants you to dream, and he expects you to plan. Most people think about having a gameplan in terms of retirement, but you ought to have goals for each stage of your life: a one-year goal, a five-year goal and even a ten-year goal.

Those of us who are married may find this hard if we are the day-to-day spouse. I (Nicole) am the day-to-day spouse, and Abidan is the visionary. I have daily, weekly, and monthly goals for our home and finances, and Abidan has goals for our family that span years and take decades to accomplish. In marriage, we need both. If both spouses are day-to-day people, or both are visionaries, it can be difficult to come up with the necessary gameplan. There needs to be balance for your planning to work. More than anything, prayer is essential for helping you develop your gameplan and achieving your dream.

Scriptures to Think On:

Cause me to know the way in which I should walk, for I lift up my soul to You. **Psalm 143:8b**

Commit your works to the Lord, and your thoughts will be established. **Proverbs 16:3**

Through wisdom a house is built, and by understanding it is established; by knowledge the rooms are filled with all precious and pleasant riches. **Proverbs 24:3-4**

For which of you, intending to build a tower, does not sit down first and count the cost, whether he has enough to finish it— lest, after he has laid the foundation, and is not able to finish, all who see it begin to mock him, saying, "This man began to build and was not able to finish.' Or what king, going to make war against another king, does not sit down first and consider whether he is able with ten thousand to meet him who comes against him with twenty thousand? Or else, while the other is still a great way off, he sends a delegation and asks conditions of peace. **Luke 14:28-32**

JOURNAL

_____

_____

_____

_____

_____

_____

_____

_____

_____

_____

_____

_____

_____

_____

_____

_____

_____

_____

12. SELF-KNOWLEDGE

Back in 2017, Nicole and I were able to go on a tour of Greece. One of our favorite sites was the Temple of Apollo in Delphi. According to Pausanias, Greek geographer and traveler, there were three maxims carved into the forecourt of the Temple, one of which said, "Know Thyself." Throughout history, people have considered self-knowledge to be a critical step towards a better, more meaningful life. But be warned—self-knowledge is not easily acquired. In *Poor Richard's Almanack*, Benjamin Franklin wrote, "There are 3 things extremely hard: steel, a diamond, and to know one's self." Although it is difficult, personal assessment is a must when it comes to reaching your goal.

Fortunately for us, the Bible gives us the secret to self-knowledge. Listen to Paul's words in Romans 12:3: "For I say, through the grace given to me, to everyone who is among you, not to think of himself more highly than he ought to think, but to think soberly, as God has dealt to each one a measure of faith."

When seeking to know yourself, always have the attitude of Paul, who humbled himself and acknowledged that his authority came only by God's grace. Secondly, recognize that it's not a sin to think of yourself. The key statement in Paul's warning is that one must not think of himself "more highly than he ought to think." In other words, approach the subject of self-knowledge with the right assessment—not too high and not too low. There's a delicate balance.

We tend to think that negative self-focus or self-talk is a sign of humility. God, however, calls it lying. He has established who you are, so be honest about your limitations as well as the gifts and abilities that he's given you. Never thinking of yourself diminishes your confidence to allow God to make positive changes in your life while also failing to acknowledge the wonder and beauty about God's own creation: you.

On the other hand, when you do begin to think on your strengths and weaknesses, be sure to give yourself a sober assessment. What do we mean by that? Well, imagine how a drunk person talks about themselves. They brag a lot. Every drunken story I've ever heard has been one of exaggerated success and conveniently forgotten shortcomings. I think back to F.B. Meyer's warning: "Don't flatter yourself when it comes to 'face or lace or place or even grace.'"

Finally, remember that your true measure is not your physical or mental strength, but your faith—not your knowledge of God, but your relationship with him. Henry Ward Beecher wisely said, "You must measure not where you touch the ground, but where you touch the sky. You must measure not the root, but the blossom; not the leaf, but the fruit." It is the size of your faith in God that determines whether or not you reach your goal.

It's not wrong to want success in life, but you must know yourself to succeed. As you begin to learn about yourself, accept what you discover. That's the only way that you can begin on the right path. It's important to know yourself, but remember that, ultimately, God is the one who knows you best. Ask him to reveal what's holding you back from moving forward.

This may be one of the hardest processes you'll ever go through. Looking at yourself with honesty can be excruciating because, oftentimes, you won't like what you see. If you aren't truly prepared by the Holy Spirit to accept what you see, you'll forever be trying to fix a false you. But you can begin right now! Today is the day to start working on your strengths and to strengthening your weaknesses. Don't just stay where you are. Find who you are in Christ!

Scriptures to Think On:

The heart is deceitful above all things, and desperately wicked; who can know it? I, the Lord, search the heart, I test the mind, even to give every man according to his ways, according to the fruit of his doings. **Jeremiah 17:9-10**

Search me, O God, and know my heart; try me, and know my anxieties; and see if there is any wicked way in me, and lead me in the way everlasting. **Psalm 139:23-24**

Examine yourselves as to whether you are in the faith. Test yourselves. Do you not know yourselves, that Jesus Christ is in you?—unless indeed you are disqualified.   **2 Corinthians 13:5**

JOURNAL

_____

_____

_____

_____

_____

_____

_____

_____

_____

_____

_____

_____

_____

_____

_____

_____

_____

13. SMALL VICTORIES

If you watch a lot of TV, you may find yourself under the impression that situations typically move from crisis to conclusion in just under an hour. That makes it hard to stomach the fact that that real life goals (relationship, financial, health, spiritual) take months, if not years, to reach. Before you cross the finish line and celebrate the great victory, take the time to look around at the many small victories God gives you along the way.

Back in 2021, I (Abidan) took my church staff on our annual retreat to Arizona. On our final day, we visited beautiful Sedona with its red rock buttes and majestic overlooks. Everyone wanted to do some hiking, so we chose the Chimney Rock Pass in the Andante Trail. The sign at the beginning of the trail read: "A rocky and exposed trail climbs up and along ledges surrounding Chimney Rock to gain the saddle between it and Capitol Butte."

How difficult could that be?

Well, we forgot that we had seven little ones with us ranging from six months to nine years old. It was fun at first, but the climb became steep in places. Those little legs started struggling. Parents had to carry younger ones, which was a little risky on the steep trail. Thank goodness, there were several places along the path to stop and catch our breath. We regularly took breaks and used the time to snap some breathtaking pictures (pun intended). The adults kept reminding their children of how far we'd come and how awesome it would be when we reached the summit! And yes, we all eventually made it to the top—it was so worth it.

So also in the trail of life, you must remember to stop, catch your breath, and take in that spectacular view of how far you've come. If you fail to celebrate the small victories and enjoy the scenery along the way, you'll lose the motivation to press toward the summit.

After God's people had crossed over the Jordan River under Joshua's leadership, they were told to take twelve stones from the riverbed and place them as markers to remind them of the incredible miracle God had done for them. Of course, the ultimate goal was much greater than simply crossing a river, but the stones were to be a "memorial to the children of Israel forever" (Joshua 4:7). In case they were tempted to retreat, the stones would always be there, a present reminder of God's faithfulness.

Even Jesus had a visit from Moses and Elijah on the Mount of Transfiguration to authenticate, and even celebrate, his journey to the cross. While the Bible doesn't tell us what these two prophets said to Jesus, God's mighty voice from heaven reverberated with approval over his Son. This moment was a pivotal milestone in Jesus' ministry, because it proved to his disciples in no uncertain terms Jesus' heavenly identity and authority. Not long afterwards, Jesus climbed that arduous hill to the cross, achieving his ultimate victory over sin and death.

What are the small goals that you can accomplish to get to your ultimate goal? Every time you reach one of those small goals, take the time to celebrate them! They're important because recognizing the accomplishment of your small goals fuels your motivation to continue towards your final goal. Small victories are also reminders of God's faithfulness along the way.

Scriptures to Think On:

Then Samuel took a stone and set it up between Mizpah and Shen, and called its name Ebenezer, saying, "Thus far the Lord has helped us."
1 Samuel 7:12

I will praise You, O Lord, with my whole heart; I will tell of all Your marvelous works.   **Psalm 9:1**

…being confident of this very thing, that He who has begun a good work in you will complete it until the day of Jesus Christ.   **Philippians 1:6**

JOURNAL

_____

_____

_____

_____

_____

_____

_____

_____

_____

_____

_____

_____

_____

_____

_____

_____

_____

_____

14. ENJOY THE PROCESS

In our fast-paced world with instant everything, people only want the result—and they want it immediately. Processes that used to be enjoyable have become tedious drudgery. We as a people have grown to despise waiting, which causes us to take shortcuts, which can lead to bad habits, and which ultimately ends in failure. Somewhere, we as a culture have forgotten that the process is a critical part of the result!

Similar mistakes were made by the Jewish people when they were first taken into the Babylonian Exile. God sent them away to purify and prepare them for the coming of the Messiah. However, somewhere along the way, they forgot that it was their own sin that caused them to be driven out in the first place. They hated the process of living in exile. All they wanted was the immediate solution—going back to Jerusalem.

God sent Jeremiah to encourage the people. Listen to Jeremiah 29:5-7: "Build houses and dwell in them; plant gardens and eat their fruit. Take wives and beget sons and daughters…and seek the peace of the city where I have caused you to be carried away captive…" In other words, God was saying, "Bloom where I've planted you. Make yourself at home. Dig some foundations. Get your hands dirty in the Babylonian soil. Become a productive member of the society. Make the place better by your presence."

At first, the people didn't want to hear that, but God was clear: this is how things would be for the next seventy years. On the other hand, if the people were obedient to plant themselves where God had placed them, then his promise to them would be this: "For I know the thoughts that I think toward you, says the Lord, thoughts of peace and not of evil, to give you a future and a hope" (Jeremiah 29:11).

People often quote this promise, but they fail to realize that God's promise was contingent on the Jewish people actually obeying him and enjoying the process he had ordained for them. True to his word, at the end of seventy years, God raised the Medo-Persian king, Cyrus the Great, to overthrow the Babylonians and free the Jewish people from their exile. As tough it was for them, the Babylonian Exile was truly a blessing in disguise. After they returned, the Jewish people finally put an end to their centuries-long struggle with idolatry once and for all. They began to study the Law, established synagogues, and became a missionary-minded people. Their journey, although difficult, placed a deep longing in their hearts for the coming of the Messiah.

How do you view your journey towards the goal God has given you? Do you dread the process? Do you complain about how difficult it is? How are the people around you being impacted for the better as you head towards your finish line? God told the Jewish people to "seek the peace of the city where I have caused you to be carried away captive, and pray to the Lord for it; for in its peace, you will have peace" (Jeremiah 29:7). In other words, your well-being is dependent on the well-being of those in your path. Do you stop to notice them along the way? Are you praying for them? Have you shared Christ with them? When you finally reach your destination, you may be surprised to find that your destination was the journey all along.

Scriptures to Think On:

Yea, though I walk through the valley of the shadow of death, I will fear no evil; For You are with me; Your rod and Your staff, they comfort me. You prepare a table before me in the presence of my enemies.
Psalm 23:4-5a

And not only that, but we also glory in tribulations, knowing that tribulation produces perseverance; and perseverance, character; and character, hope.
Romans 5:3-4

Then one of the elders answered, saying to me, "Who are these arrayed in white robes, and where did they come from?" And I said to him, "Sir, you know." So he said to me, "These are the ones who come out of the great tribulation, and washed their robes and made them white in the blood of the Lamb. Therefore, they are before the throne of God, and serve him day and night in his temple. And He who sits on the throne will dwell among them. They shall neither hunger anymore nor thirst anymore; the sun shall not strike them, nor any heat; for the Lamb who is in the midst of the throne will shepherd them and lead them to living fountains of waters. And God will wipe away every tear from their eyes." **Revelation 7:13-17**

JOURNAL

_____

_____

_____

_____

_____

_____

_____

_____

_____

_____

_____

_____

_____

_____

_____

_____

_____

15. THEME

If you've ever set a practical goal for yourself, you're probably familiar with the feeling of not completing it. We fall short of our goal and chalk the whole experience up to failure. But is it, really? Think about it—if you resolve to read your Bible for ten days straight, but you only do it for nine, have you really failed? You still read your Bible for nine days straight! The wisdom and guidance you've gleaned from your time spent in the Word still benefits you whether or not you were faithful to read on that tenth day.

The simple truth is that human behavior is extremely difficult—if not impossible—to change without God's guidance. To accomplish their desired outcomes, many people have taken to adopting an overarching theme rather than establishing hard-and-fast goals. Instead of setting themselves up to fail with, "I will read the Bible every day this year," they allow that year to be their "year of Bible-reading." Sure, they may not get through the entire Bible or read it every single day without fail, but on the whole, they are reading the Bible much more than they otherwise would have!

Keep in mind, setting goals for yourself is not bad. Setting concrete markers of progress for yourself is actually a good thing. But themes are also very helpful because they are broad ways to accomplish your goals a little bit at a time. Often, people will choose a "theme verse" that they take with them throughout the year. Others adopt a word such as, "grateful," "obedient", "surrender", etc.

When you choose a theme verse, pick something that has a meaningful, broad navigation toward where you want your life to go. Write it down some place where you'll see it every day. Then, strive to make that verse real in your life with God's help. When you're sitting around with nothing to do, meditate on it. When unexpected challenges pop up in your life, work to be obedient to that verse. At the end of the year, evaluate how you lived out that verse. The same goes for any word that you may adopt for the year. If your theme word is "grace," find small ways to illustrate grace every day. If it's "patience", find ways in which you can show patience, or even help others to be patient! Whether you choose a verse or a word (or both!) to be your theme, it needs to become your mindset through the Holy Spirit.

Here are a couple of examples of verses that inspired great men and women of God:

- Martin Luther (German reformer) – "as it is written, 'The just shall live by faith'" (Romans 1:17).
- Harriet Beecher Stowe (author and abolitionist) – "No longer do I call you servants, for a servant does not know what his master is doing; but I have called you friends…" (John 15:15).
- Charles Spurgeon (Baptist preacher) – "Look to Me, and be saved, all you ends of the earth!

For I am God, and there is no other" (Isaiah 45:22).

- Joni Eareckson Tada (Founder and CEO of Joni and Friends International Disability Center) – "And we know that all things work together for good to those who love God, to those who are the called according to His purpose" (Romans 8:28).

- C. S. Lewis (writer and apologist) – "And God said to Moses, 'I AM WHO I AM.' And he said, "Thus you shall say to the children of Israel, 'I AM has sent me to you'" (Exodus 3:14).

- Corrie Ten Boom (helped Jewish people escape the Nazis) – "He who dwells in the secret place of the Most High shall abide under the shadow of the Almighty" (Psalm 91:1).

- Booker T. Washington (author of "Up from Slavery" and first principal of Tuskegee Institute) – "He who overcomes shall be clothed in white garments" (Revelation 3:5a).

Your theme verse or word needs to become so ingrained in your life that it becomes the plumb line for your every action. What is your life verse or word for this year? If you don't have one, don't stress! You don't have to wait until the beginning of the year to get started. You can choose a verse or word and start living it out right now. Take today to decide on yours, and if you can't think of one, pray and ask God to give you one, and then, with his help, live accordingly!

Scriptures to Think On:

Oh, taste and see that the Lord is good; Blessed is the man who trusts in him! **Psalm 34:8**

Trust in the Lord with all your heart, and lean not on your own understanding; In all your ways acknowledge him, and he shall direct your paths. **Proverbs 3:5-6**

Fear not, for I am with you; be not dismayed, for I am your God. I will strengthen you, yes, I will help you, I will uphold you with My righteous right hand. **Isaiah 41:10**

Therefore do not worry about tomorrow, for tomorrow will worry about its own things. Sufficient for the day is its own trouble. **Matthew 6:34**

Pursue peace with all people, and holiness, without which no one will see the Lord. **Hebrews 12:14**

JOURNAL

_____

_____

_____

_____

_____

_____

_____

_____

_____

_____

_____

_____

_____

_____

_____

_____

_____

16. PATIENCE

Making a fresh start takes patience. You can't just snap your fingers and find yourself at the finish line. It's a process. Life has many unexpected situations that will derail you, discourage you, and even demoralize you. In those situations, patience is, ironically enough, what keeps you moving forward.

The paragon of patience in the Bible is Job. He was "blameless and upright, and one who feared God and shunned evil" (Job 1:1). He had a wonderful family—seven sons and three daughters—and an abundance of riches. One day, Satan got permission from God to test Job. In twenty-four hours, Job's entire world was turned upside down. The Sabeans raided his farm and stole his oxen and donkeys and killed the servants; fire fell from heaven on his sheep and the servants keeping them; the Chaldeans stole all his camels and killed the servants; finally, a great wind destroyed his house, killing all his children. He lost everything. And if that weren't enough, Satan even got permission from God to attack Job with blistering boils all over his body.

When Job's wife saw him sitting in ashes, scratching himself with a shard of pottery, she felt sorry for him and advised him to curse God and die. Job responded with, "'Shall we indeed accept good from God, and shall we not accept adversity?' In all this, Job did not sin with his lips" (Job 2:10bc).

His friends came to console him, but ended up accusing him of some unconfessed sin in his life, ultimately making him feel worse. Job was truly at rock bottom. With his faith running low, he certainly went through moments of discouragement. He was doubtful of God's character and even said things regarding the justice of God and about putting God on trial.

Nonetheless, Job never lost his integrity. In fact, he clung to it tightly, as he declared, "My lips will not speak wickedness, nor my tongue utter deceit. Far be it from me that I should say you are right; till I die I will not put away my integrity from me" (Job 27:4-5).

What was the secret to Job's final vindication and the special care of God in his life? The answer is actually found in the New Testament, in the book of James: "Indeed we count them blessed who endure. You have heard of the perseverance of Job and seen the end intended by the Lord—that the Lord is very compassionate and merciful" (James 5:11). In essence, Job's secret to God's blessing in his life was patience.

As you press on, patience will become more and more critical the closer you get to the finish line. Along with the challenges that come with your goal, there will also be unexpected problems in your life. Keep your eyes on the prize, but don't forget to concentrate on the small steps as well.

Periodically, take stock of where you are in the process. If you're constantly looking at the end goal, you may get impatient or discouraged, especially when unexpected challenges start to overwhelm you. This is because you can't accurately see your progress. When you reach one of your small goals, take the time to reflect on where you started from and where you're going. Focus on how God has moved in your life, especially through these unexpected situations. Take time to thank him for working on your behalf. God will finish what he has started in your life. Continue to seek him each day as you begin anew and be aware of his leading in your life.

Scriptures to Think On:

I waited patiently for the Lord; and he inclined to me, and heard my cry. He also brought me up out of a horrible pit, out of the miry clay, and set my feet upon a rock, and established my steps. He has put a new song in my mouth—Praise to our God; many will see it and fear, and will trust in the Lord. **Psalm 40:1-2**

The end of a thing is better than its beginning; the patient in spirit is better than the proud in spirit. **Ecclesiastes 7:8**

and not only that, but we also glory in tribulations, knowing that tribulation produces perseverance; and perseverance, character; and character, hope. **Romans 5:3-4**

Rejoicing in hope, patient in tribulation, continuing steadfastly in prayer; **Romans 12:12**

JOURNAL

_____

_____

_____

_____

_____

_____

_____

_____

_____

_____

_____

_____

_____

_____

_____

_____

_____

17. FIND STRENGTH IN GOD

Nicole and I been working out for several years now. It's always encouraging to go into the gym and lift heavier weights than we did a few months ago or run an extra ten minutes on the elliptical than we did last week. It's a sign that we're getting stronger! But true strength is much more than just muscular strength or endurance. It's our resolve in the face of incredible odds to press forward and complete the goal that God has laid on our hearts. Strength is a state of mind.

Only a year after freeing the people of Israel from Egypt, God brought them to Kadesh Barnea on the southern end of the Promised Land. Then, Moses sent in twelve men to spy out the land, one from each tribe of Israel. Ten of them returned with an evil report of a devouring land with giants! These men discouraged the hearts of the people, even referring to themselves as grasshoppers! But the last two spies, Joshua and Caleb, tried to encourage the people to immediately go forward, referring to the people of the land as "our bread." Regardless of their pleas, the people listened to the ten spies and even threatened to stone the two faithful ones. God's punishment for their faithlessness was for the people to wander in the wilderness for forty years until that unfaithful generation (twenty years old and above) died—all except for Joshua and Caleb.

Now, fast forward forty-five years: the second generation is finally in the land under Joshua's leadership. Caleb is eighty-five years old. As a side note, sometimes we wrongly believe that people in biblical times lived hundreds of years, assuming that their eighty was equivalent to our forty. Not true. In the antediluvian age (the age before the deluge/flood), people did live hundreds of years (Adam lived nine-hundred-thirty years, Methuselah lived nine-hundred and sixty-nine!), but after the flood, the age of human beings dropped to about the same as our times. Listen to Moses' words in Psalm 90:10—"The days of our lives are seventy years; and if by reason of strength they are eighty years, yet their boast is only labor and sorrow; or it is soon cut off, and we fly away."

All this goes to say that Caleb was no spring chicken! Nonetheless, he said to Joshua, "Behold, the Lord has kept me alive, as he said, these forty-five years, ever since the Lord spoke this word to Moses while Israel wandered in the wilderness; and now, here I am this day, eighty-five years old. As yet I am as strong this day as on the day that Moses sent me; just as my strength was then, so now is my strength for war, both for going out and for coming in. Now therefore, give me this mountain of which the Lord spoke in that day" (Joshua 14:6-12).

Caleb's strength was more than just physical strength. It was his resolve in God's promise!

Picture your end goal and think about the progress you've made so far. Have you been trying to accomplish it in your own strength? That makes the process much more difficult. It'll always feel like you take one step forward and two steps back. Don't forget, when you got saved, the Holy Spirit came to live within you. You have his power to rely on. The problem is that we sometimes continue to operate in our own power, which is unreliable and always ends up failing. If you want a fresh start, leave all your worries and trouble with the Lord. He's strong enough to handle it. God doesn't want you to get saved just to live life on your own. He wants to lead you and guide you. He wants to go on your journey with you. He will never leave you nor forsake you; All you need to do is invite him along. And his promise remains: "My grace is sufficient for you, for my strength is made perfect in weakness" (2 Corinthians 12:9a).

Scriptures to Think On:

God is my strength and power, and he makes my way perfect. **2 Samuel 22:33**

Do not sorrow, for the joy of the Lord is your strength. **Nehemiah 8:10d**

I will love You, O Lord, my strength. The Lord is my rock and my fortress and my deliverer; My God, my strength, in whom I will trust... **Psalm 18:1-2**

For when we were still without strength, in due time Christ died for the ungodly. **Romans 5:6**

JOURNAL

_____

_____

_____

_____

_____

_____

_____

_____

_____

_____

_____

_____

_____

_____

_____

_____

_____

18. SELF-TALK

There's only one thing that feels worse than someone talking down to you—talking down to yourself! Words are powerful, especially when they're directed towards your own self. They can make or break you. Believe it or not, how you talk to yourself can be the missing ingredient or the stumbling block that keeps you from achieving your goal.

The Bible has a lot to say about words, albeit the focus is on how you use them in addressing others. But if the second greatest commandment is, "You shall love your neighbor as yourself," then loving oneself properly is an important prerequisite to loving your neighbor. To talk degradingly and negatively to yourself but encouragingly to others is not only unhelpful, but also hypocritical.

James reminds us, "Out of the same mouth proceed blessing and cursing. My brethren, these things ought not to be so. Does a spring send forth fresh water and bitter from the same opening? Can a fig tree, my brethren, bear olives, or a grapevine bear figs? Thus, no spring yields both salt water and fresh." (James 3:10-12).

There are examples in the Bible of both positive and negative self-talk. In Genesis, God reminded Abraham of his promise to send him a son even though he was ninety-nine years old and Sarah eighty-nine. Remember Abraham's response? The Bible says he "fell on his face and laughed, and said in his heart, 'Shall a child be born to a man who is one hundred years old? And shall Sarah, who is ninety years old, bear a child?'" (Genesis 17:17). Only God's grace overlooked Abraham's negative self-talk, and, the following year, Isaac was born!

On the other hand, when the Prodigal Son had a moment of self-realization, he said, "How many of my father's hired servants have bread enough and to spare, and I perish with hunger! I will arise and go to my father, and will say to him, 'Father, I have sinned against heaven and before you, and I am no longer worthy to be called your son. Make me like one of your hired servants' And he arose and came to his father" (Luke 15:17-20). If the Prodigal Son had spoken negatively of his father and continued eating the swine's pods, he'd have never experienced the blessing of returning home, being forgiven by his father, and being restored to his fullness.

Your inner dialogue is very important. For most of us—especially women—it's overwhelmingly negative. What we tell ourselves often stems from internalizing things that we have been told by others for many years. That's why it's so important to surround yourself with godly people who will speak truth to you. Your inner dialogue sets the course for your life.

Take some time today to reflect on your conversation with yourself. Do you like the world that you've spoken into existence? If not, start by changing your self-talk. It's a difficult habit to change but start small. The Bible has so many things to say about you that are positive and uplifting: You are God's masterpiece. You are God's special treasure. You are God's child if you are born again. The next time you begin the negative diatribe in your head, stop and say about yourself what God says about you. This might just get you moving towards your goal.

Scriptures to Think On:

Why are you cast down, O my soul? And why are you disquieted within me? Hope in God, for I shall yet praise him for the help of his countenance.
Psalm 42:5

Bless the Lord, O my soul; and all that is within me, bless his holy name! Bless the Lord, O my soul, and forget not all his benefits: Who forgives all your iniquities, who heals all your diseases, who redeems your life from destruction, who crowns you with lovingkindness and tender mercies, who satisfies your mouth with good things, so that your youth is renewed like the eagle's. **Psalm 103:1-5**

And suddenly, a woman who had a flow of blood for twelve years came from behind and touched the hem of his garment. For she said to herself, "If only I may touch his garment, I shall be made well." But Jesus turned around, and when he saw her, he said, "Be of good cheer, daughter; your faith has made you well." And the woman was made well from that hour.
Matthew 9:20-22

JOURNAL

_____

_____

_____

_____

_____

_____

_____

_____

_____

_____

_____

_____

_____

_____

_____

_____

19. FRIENDSHIPS

"A man is known by the company he keeps," said the philosopher Aesop. Although he lived about 2,500 years ago, his statement is as true today as it was back then. Take a good look at your friend circle. If other people were to look at them, what would they think of you? Would they see someone who walks with integrity, or would they see a hypocrite? Would they see someone who is focused and determined, or someone who is flighty and wavering? Would they see someone who will achieve great things for the kingdom of God, or someone who lives only for self? However you answer those questions, you can be sure that that's how you appear to the people around you.

I would actually take Aesop's quote one step further to say, "A man's *success* is determined by the company he keeps." The sad truth is no matter what you do in life, there will always be those who don't want to see you succeed. Sometimes, those people are the ones closest to you. How do your friends respond to your goal? Are they even aware that you're on a path to a new beginning? If so, do they encourage you to press on? What is their reaction to your success? If your friends seem resentful or dismissive when you succeed in life, then they are not truly your friends. True friends rejoice with you when you succeed. If you are seeking to make a new beginning or achieve a new goal, you need to take a good look at who your friends are to see whether they are cheering you on or not. If not, you're better off without them.

Think about King David. Before he took the throne, his best friend was Jonathan, the son of Saul, the king of Israel—and David's sworn enemy. Their friendship may have begun right after David killed Goliath, or even earlier when David would visit the palace and play his harp to soothe Saul's distress. 1 Samuel 18:1-4 describes their friendship so beautifully: "the soul of Jonathan was knit to the soul of David, and Jonathan loved him as his own soul...Then Jonathan and David made a covenant, because he loved him as his own soul. And Jonathan took off the robe that was on him and gave it to David, with his armor, even to his sword and his bow and his belt."

At first, Saul was also grateful for David's presence in his life, but in time, he began to resent the young man. Saul even tried to kill David by throwing a javelin at him! When Jonathan perceived what his father was plotting, he warned David and tried to speak to his father on David's behalf. Things calmed down for a while, but eventually, Saul's insecurity got the better of him. In fact, when Jonathan warned David that his life was in danger, Saul cast a spear at his own son!

At the end of the day, Jonathan knew that David was God's chosen king. The two friends made a covenant with each other saying, "May the Lord be between you and me, and between your descendants and my descendants, forever." When Jonathan was killed in battle, David kept his end of their pact when he made Jonathan's son, Mephibosheth, stay in his palace and sit at his dinner table. What a marvelous example of a godly—if unlikely—friendship!

Do you have a faithful friend like Jonathan in your life? Are you a faithful friend like David was to Jonathan? You may also want to prayerfully build a community of like-minded friends who will encourage you to follow God's plan for a new beginning. Think of David's mighty men in 2 Samuel 23:8-39 and 1 Chronicles 11:10-47. They were the toughest military warriors in history. One killed eight hundred men in one battle and another went into a pit and killed a lion on a snowy day! Imagine such friends being your cheerleaders!

Scriptures to Think On:

Now when Job's three friends heard of all this adversity that had come upon him, each one came from his own place. **Job 2:11**

The righteous should choose his friends carefully, For the way of the wicked leads them astray.
Proverbs 12:26

A man who has friends must himself be friendly…
Proverbs 18:24

As iron sharpens iron, so a man sharpens the countenance of his friend. **Proverbs 27:17**

Greater love has no one than this, than to lay down one's life for his friends. You are My friends if you do whatever I command you. No longer do I call you servants, for a servant does not know what his master is doing; but I have called you friends, for all things that I heard from My Father I have made known to you. **John 15:13-15**

JOURNAL

_____

_____

_____

_____

_____

_____

_____

_____

_____

_____

_____

_____

_____

20. PESSIMISM

Are you a person that sees the glass half-empty or half-full? Optimists typically see the good in situations around them, confident and hopeful for what their future holds. Pessimists, by contrast, tend to see the negative aspects of life, choosing to focus on things that can and, in their minds, will inevitably go wrong.

If you're unsure which you are, think back to the feedback you've received from friends and family. Sometimes, we claim to be realists when we're really wallowing in pessimism. True realistic thinkers, however, understand the facts of their situation and make decisions based on those facts. Pessimism and optimism simply represent the attitudes in which we react to life's situations.

If anyone had an excuse to be pessimistic, it was the Apostle Paul, especially in the final years of his life. We find evidence for this in his last letter written to Timothy, his son in the ministry. To be specific, Paul was about to be beheaded on the Ostian Way in Rome at the hands of Nero, the wicked Roman emperor. Talk about a negative situation!

Listen to some of the portions of the letter and notice how many of Paul's earlier partners in ministry had abandoned him:

- "This you know, that all those in Asia have turned away from me, among whom are Phygellus and Hermogenes" (2 Timothy 1:15).
- "But shun profane and idle babblings, for they will increase to more ungodliness. And their message will spread like cancer. Hymenaeus and Philetus are of this sort, who have strayed concerning the truth" (2 Timothy 2:16-18a).
- "Be diligent to come to me quickly; for Demas has forsaken me, having loved this present world, and has departed for Thessalonica—Crescens for Galatia, Titus for Dalmatia" (2 Timothy 4:9).
- "Alexander the coppersmith did me much harm. May the Lord repay him according to his works. You also must beware of him, for he has greatly resisted our words" (2 Timothy 4:14-15).
- "At my first defense no one stood with me, but all forsook me" (2 Timothy 4:16a).

We can't be completely sure from the context whether Hymenaeus, Philetus, and Alexander were Paul's companions or just acquaintances—nonetheless, it must have been heartbreaking for the old missionary to see so many of his friends fading away from him in his final hours. But instead of becoming disheartened, note how Paul was full of resolve and optimism for the future of ministry:

- "For God has not given us a spirit of fear, but of power and of love and of a sound mind" (2 Timothy 1:7).

- "I am not ashamed, for I know whom I have believed and am persuaded that he is able to keep what I have committed to him until that Day" (2 Timothy 1:12).
- "I have fought the good fight, I have finished the race, I have kept the faith. Finally, there is laid up for me the crown of righteousness" (2 Timothy 4:7-8a).
- "And the Lord will deliver me from every evil work and preserve me for his heavenly kingdom" (2 Timothy 4:18).

God is our hope and our salvation! If you believe this to be true, then there is no room for pessimism in your life. You can approach life both realistically and optimistically, believing that God is working everything for your good and his glory. There is a quote by Elisabeth Elliot in her book, *On Asking God Why*, that really helps put life into perspective—"God will never protect you from anything that will make you more like Jesus." Just like Paul, you can be confident that whatever is happening in your life is coming through the hand of God!

Scriptures to Think On:

Through the Lord's mercies we are not consumed, because his compassions fail not. They are new every morning; Great is Your faithfulness.
Lamentations 3:22-23

I have set the Lord always before me; because he is at my right hand I shall not be moved. Therefore my heart is glad, and my glory rejoices; my flesh also will rest in hope. **Psalm 16:8-9**

In the world you will have tribulation; but be of good cheer, I have overcome the world. **John 16:33b**

For I consider that the sufferings of this present time are not worthy to be compared with the glory which shall be revealed in us. **Romans 8:18**

JOURNAL

21. LOOK AT FAILURE THE RIGHT WAY

Anything worth doing always carries with it the potential, or even promise, of failure. Unfortunately, most people consider failure to be a proof that whatever they were attempting was never meant to be. To the contrary, failure is simply narrowing down your options of how to achieve your goal.

When Thomas Edison was working on a new type of nickel-iron storage battery, his corps of chemists and engineers made hundreds of little test cells. After conducting as many as nine thousand experiments, Edison was forced to admit the truth: none of them worked. Walter Mallory, his long-time associate, saw all the failed attempts and remarked sympathetically, "Isn't it a shame that with the tremendous amount of work you have done, you haven't been able to get any results?"

To this, Edison responded, "Results! Why, man, I have gotten a lot of results! I know several thousand things that won't work."

Moses is a perfect example of biblical failure. As the Exodus account goes, he was raised by the Pharaoh's daughter, but when he came of age, his heart went out to his people. When he saw an Egyptian beating a Hebrew, Moses intervened, killing the Egyptian and hiding his body in the sand. Of course, word got out. When Moses tried to intervene between two Hebrews fighting with each other, the one who was at wrong taunted him, "Who made you a prince and a judge over us? Do you intend to kill me as you killed the Egyptian?"

When Moses heard that, fear came into his heart. After learning that Pharaoh wanted to kill him, he fled to Midian. In his own eyes, Moses probably felt like a failure. However, the Bible never condemns Moses' action as sin. God knew Moses was a work in progress, merely ahead of his time. The people weren't yet ready to be freed, and Moses was not yet ready to lead them. It would take another forty years for their cry to come up to God and for Moses to learn how to be a shepherd.

John Maxwell, in his book *Failing Forward: Turning Mistakes into Stepping Stones for Success*, makes a powerful statement: "The difference between average people and achieving people is their perception of and response to failure." Maxwell goes on to share the story of Erma Bombeck, a famous newspaper humor columnist, who had to face tough challenges ranging from breast cancer to kidney failure. She knew how to handle failure—"What you have to tell yourself is, 'I'm not a failure. I failed at doing something.' There's a big difference."

How do you see failure in your life? When you don't succeed, do you stop trying? If so, why not pick yourself up and ask yourself what you've learned? Failing is a fantastic opportunity to learn what works and what doesn't. You can throw yourself a pity party or you can be willing to learn and grow from your failures!

You can also learn a lot about yourself during these times if you're willing to be introspective. Never forget that during these times, God is using your attempts and your failings to refine you and to teach you something about himself—or even about yourself. God is constantly at work in your life, and He's working even through your failings. Be willing to learn and to grow from the good and the bad experiences.

Scriptures to Think On:

The steps of a good man are ordered by the Lord, and He delights in his way. Though he fall, he shall not be utterly cast down; for the Lord upholds him with his hand. **Psalm 37:23-24**

For a righteous man may fall seven times and rise again… **Proverbs 24:16a**

But we have this treasure in earthen vessels, that the excellence of the power may be of God and not of us. We are hard-pressed on every side, yet not crushed; we are perplexed, but not in despair; persecuted, but not forsaken; struck down, but not destroyed.
2 Corinthians 4:7-9

JOURNAL

_____

_____

_____

_____

_____

_____

_____

_____

_____

_____

_____

_____

_____

_____

_____

_____

_____

22. IMPACT ON LOVED ONES

When we traveled with our kids in their younger days, we always made sure the hotels where we stayed had a swimming pool. They loved it (especially the boys), but we had to remind them to be mindful of who was around the pool before they cannon-balled in. We would tell them: "Just because you're having a great time doesn't mean that others want to get splashed."

That advice also applies to those who are seeking a new beginning. Be mindful of those around you. Don't let your high moments be low moments for your loved ones along the journey.

God called Abraham saying, "Get out of your country, from your family and from your father's house, to a land that I will show you. I will make you a great nation; I will bless you and make your name great; and you shall be a blessing. I will bless those who bless you, and I will curse him who curses you; and in you all the families of the earth shall be blessed" (Genesis 12:1-3).

This was a calling for Abraham to be the family line through which the Son of God would one day come to redeem the sins of the world. Abraham assumed that this calling was only for him, and not his wife Sarah, and that it was going to be his descendant who would one day be a blessing to the nations.

His actions towards Sarah prove that this was a foolish assumption. For starters, he made an unholy pact with her before they fled to Egypt to escape famine. "Indeed, I know that you are a woman of beautiful countenance. Therefore, it will happen, when the Egyptians see you, that they will say, 'This is his wife'; and they will kill me, but they will let you live. Please say you are my sister, that it may be well with me for your sake, and that I may live because of you" (Genesis 12:11b-13).

God intervened and saved Sarah, but not before plaguing Pharaoh and his household. Then later, as time passed and no child was born to Sarah, she offered her maidservant, Hagar, to Abraham, and he took her. However, the son born, Ishmael, was not God's promised one. As Abraham neared ninety-nine years of age (and Sarah eighty-nine), he made the same mistake that he had made earlier with Pharaoh—this time with Abimelech, king of Gerar. Again, God had to step in and protect Sarah.

After reaching the age of ninety, Sarah finally gave birth to Isaac, the son God had promised. In retrospect, the root cause of each of their failures was Abraham's false assumption that God's plan involved only him and not Sarah. He forgot that even though God had called him specifically, it was the seed of the woman who would crush the head of the serpent (Genesis 3:15).

As you are moving forward in your fresh start, make sure your family is on board with you. There must be conversations with your family about your plans and your goals as you begin your new journey, because they will undoubtedly be affected by them—even if those changes are for the better. You chose to do life with your spouse, so don't leave them behind. If you have children, they'll also be affected by your decisions. Even if they are young, explain to them what is happening on their level so they can understand and be on the same team. To accomplish your goals, you'll need support. Your family is God's first line of support for you, because they love you and should want to see you succeed. Be sure to involve them in every step along the way!

Scriptures to Think On:

Therefore, a man shall leave his father and mother and be joined to his wife, and they shall become one flesh. **Genesis 2:24**

And if it seems evil to you to serve the Lord, choose for yourselves this day whom you will serve...But as for me and my house, we will serve the Lord. **Joshua 24:15**

He who is greedy for gain troubles his own house... **Proverbs 15:27a**

But if anyone does not provide for his own, and especially for those of his household, he has denied the faith and is worse than an unbeliever.   **1 Timothy 5:8**

JOURNAL

_____

_____

_____

_____

_____

_____

_____

_____

_____

_____

_____

_____

_____

_____

_____

_____

_____

23. AVOID JEALOUSY AND ENVY

People often associate certain colors with certain moods, emotions, or attitudes:

> Red—Anger
> Blue—Sadness/Peace
> Yellow—Fear/Weakness
> Gold—Wealth
> Purple—Royalty/Pride
> Green—Jealousy/Envy

In Western society, we even call envy "The Green-Eyed Monster" because green is a color typically associated with sickness. Sometimes, when people fall ill, their skin takes on a slightly yellowish-green tinge. So also, when a person is infected with jealousy or envy, their countenance takes on a sick appearance.

It's interesting, then, that the Hebrew word for jealousy or envy in the Old Testament is *kanah*, which is literally "to become intensely red." Unlike our western context that sees jealousy and envy as something sickening, the semitic context depicts it as passionate and fiery.

Additionally, when the Jewish people translated their Hebrew Bible into Greek—called the Septuagint—they translated *kanah* with *zelou*, which literally means "to burn" or "to boil." It can have a positive or a negative meaning. Positively, it means to "deeply desire," "eagerly desire," or "zealously strive." It's like when we say, "he was burning with energy" or "she was burning with excitement." But this same word can also have a negative connotation. Sometimes it can mean jealousy, and other times it can mean envy. Either way, both the Hebrew and the Greek words indicate that passion left unguarded can slip into jealousy or envy.

Furthermore, there is a distinct difference between jealousy and envy. Jealousy is when you have something that you will not share with someone. For example, a jealous boyfriend or girlfriend is unwilling to share their partner with anyone else. On the other hand, envy is when you want something that someone else has, and you resent them for it. God is jealous over us, but he is not envious of us. Jealousy is possessive, envy is resentful. Either way, when you are driving towards a goal, it can be easy to fall into one or the other. We can become jealous, refusing to share our knowledge with someone in need of encouragement or help. We can also become envious, resenting someone further in life than we are and wishing them ill. Both are detrimental in different ways to our life and well-being.

So, how do you combat jealousy and envy as you're seeking a new beginning or trying to reach your goal? Every day, remind yourself of God's grace and goodness in your life. Everything you are and everything you have achieved is a gift from God. Genuine gratitude for God's blessings will guard you from becoming jealous. Complimenting and encouraging others on their success will protect you from becoming envious. Avoid the pitfall of comparing yourself to the success of others—in fact, go out of your way to help them! Doing this will prevent jealousy or envy from finding any foothold in your life. In turn, you will have a healthy countenance as you passionately pursue your own new beginnings!

Scriptures to Think On:

Wrath is cruel and anger a torrent, but who is able to stand before jealousy? **Proverbs 27:4**

I thank You and praise You, O God of my fathers; You have given me wisdom and might, and have now made known to me what we asked of You, For You have made known to us the king's demand. **Daniel 2:23**

Love suffers long and is kind; love does not envy; love does not parade itself, is not puffed up.
1 Corinthians 13:4

Therefore, laying aside all malice, all deceit, hypocrisy, envy, and all evil speaking, as newborn babes, desire the pure milk of the word, that you may grow thereby, if indeed you have tasted that the Lord is gracious. **1 Peter 2:1-2**

JOURNAL

24. SEEING POSSIBILITIES

Throughout history, most major discoveries and inventions began with seeds of discontent and inconvenience. To quote leadership expert John C. Maxwell, "Discontent with the status quo is a great catalyst for vision." In other words, if you're content with how things are, you will never aspire to anything more.

Take Nehemiah for example. He was a Jewish man serving the King of Persia as a cupbearer—an extremely prominent position. One day, he received terrible news of his people's plight in Jerusalem. The walls of the city had been broken down and the gates were burned with fire. Nehemiah was deeply moved; the seed of his discontent was now firmly planted in his heart. He fasted and prayed for many days, finally mustering the courage to go before the king. Amazingly, the king promised to help him with everything he needed! In Nehemiah's own words: "the king granted them to me according to the good hand of my God upon me" (Nehemiah 2:8).

With that assurance, Nehemiah set off on a seven-hundred-mile journey toward Jerusalem. You can imagine how exhausted he must've been when he arrived! After just three days of rest, he arose in the night and went to survey the destruction. He only took a handful of men with him, careful not to tell anyone what God had put in his heart. There's another lesson for all of us: When God gives you a goal, be very careful who you share it with. If you share your vision with the wrong people, they will try to quench it or even sabotage it. In time, Nehemiah shared his goal with his people, and they immediately went to work.

Unfortunately, Nehemiah encountered detractors along the way. "But when Sanballat the Horonite, Tobiah the Ammonite official, and Geshem the Arab heard of it, they laughed at us and despised us, and said, 'What is this thing that you are doing? Will you rebel against the king?'" (Nehemiah 2:19).

These three men were the rulers of surrounding regions, threatened by the renewed hope of God's people. Keep this in mind—any time you attempt to accomplish a goal worth achieving, expect to face opposition. Jerry Falwell, the founder of Liberty University, once said, "You do not determine a person's greatness by their talent or wealth, as the world does, but rather by what it takes to discourage them." Nehemiah refused to be discouraged or intimated and kept his eyes on the vision, and, in only fifty-two days, the walls around Jerusalem were completed!

As you've been going through the process of beginning anew, can you identify the source of discontent in your life? Has God given you a vision for where he wants you to go? Look for the possibilities that God is placing in your life. Ask him for wisdom to make the right choices. The Bible is full of "If...then" promises. If we are obedient to what God wants us to do, then he will do what he's promised.

So many people wonder what God's vision is for

their lives, or when he will reveal it to them. It's really very simple! God's vision for your life is for you to glorify him in all that you do. Ask God to show you the possibilities that he is laying out for you. Then, get ready, because he will be faithful to show you if you ask!

Scriptures to Think On:

Delight yourself also in the Lord, and he shall give you the desires of your heart. Commit your way to the Lord, trust also in him, and he shall bring it to pass. **Psalm 37:4-5**

Commit your works to the Lord, and your thoughts will be established.   **Proverbs 16:3**

And he would gladly have filled his stomach with the pods that the swine ate, and no one gave him anything. "But when he came to himself, he said, 'How many of my father's hired servants have bread enough and to spare, and I perish with hunger! I will arise and go to my father...'"   **Luke 15:16-18a**

For we are his workmanship, created in Christ Jesus for good works, which God prepared beforehand that we should walk in them.   **Ephesians 2:10**

JOURNAL

_____

_____

_____

_____

_____

_____

_____

_____

_____

_____

_____

_____

_____

_____

_____

_____

25. LEARN FROM OTHERS

"Being original is overrated." I (Abidan) tried to find the original source of that statement but eventually gave up. As with all great quotes, there are simply too many variations to choose from!

In all seriousness, some people strive to be original by charting their own course and reaching their vision through the school of hard knocks. If only they would look down the path, they'd find that someone else has already cleared the way for them. Why not learn from them? After all, "Imitation is the sincerest form of flattery!" (I tried to find the original source of that statement too but gave up again. The true author may just have to imagine my compliments.)

The Bible has a lot to say about the value of learning from others. Lot followed Abraham, his uncle, into the Promised Land. Moses was mentored by his father-in-law, Jethro, in how to delegate the burden of judging the people. Joshua was an assistant to Moses and followed in his footsteps. Ruth was mentored by Naomi, her mother-in-law. King Saul failed to learn from Samuel, the prophet who anointed him, but David remained teachable, as seen in Nathan's confrontation of David. Elisha was mentored by Elijah, who even left Elisha the mantle and the double portion of his spirit to do miracles. In the New

Testament, Jesus mentored his disciples to do "greater works than these." Timothy was instructed by Paul, who even referred to him as his "true son in the faith" (1 Timothy 1:2). Aquila and Priscilla took Apollos aside and "explained to him the way of God more accurately" (Acts 18:26). And the beautiful thing is, in most of these relationships, the mentee superseded the mentor in effectiveness!

In learning from others, it also helps to remember that while millions have succeeded before you, millions more have failed. Remember the quote from Winston Churchill: "Success is not final. Failure is not fatal. It is the courage to continue that counts."

Failing is an inevitable part of life, but it doesn't have to be all bad. Failure provides an opportunity to learn what works and what doesn't. And the best part is, you don't have to only learn from your failures. Never be envious of those who've walked the road before you—they can be your greatest teachers. Learn from their mistakes and make the proper corrections.

It takes determination and perseverance to continue pursuing your goal. If you give up, you'll fall short of the joy that others have gained from reaching their own goals. And always remember that it doesn't end with you—God is setting you up to be an example for those coming behind you as well! The lessons you're learning now will become the footholds for others to climb the summit behind you.

Scriptures to Think On:

One generation shall praise Your works to another, and shall declare Your mighty acts.   **Psalm 145:4**

My son, hear the instruction of your father, and do not forsake the law of your mother; For they will be a graceful ornament on your head, and chains about your neck.   **Proverbs 1:8-9**

Give instruction to a wise man, and he will be still wiser; teach a just man, and he will increase in learning. **Proverbs 9:9**

Plans are established by counsel; By wise counsel wage war.   **Proverbs 20:18**

Imitate me, just as I also imitate Christ.
1 Corinthians 11:1

The things which you learned and received and heard and saw in me, these do, and the God of peace will be with you.   **Philippians 4:9**

JOURNAL

_____

_____

_____

_____

_____

_____

_____

_____

_____

_____

_____

_____

_____

_____

_____

_____

_____

26. FALSE HOPE

You would be surprised how many people suffer from the "If-Only Syndrome."

"If only I had _____, I could reach my goal."

"If only I lived _____, I'd be able to achieve my dream."

"If only I knew _____, I'd be so far ahead."

Statements like these are built on the assumption that a location, thing, or person is the key to reaching one's goal. Although certain essentials are required in reaching a goal, these factors should never become an excuse for inactivity or apathy.

A change of scenery is nice, but it's no silver bullet to success. A new address on your mailbox can't solve the deep-rooted problems that sparked your journey toward a fresh start. Even if you change locations, you'll still be the same person.

Think about Daniel, who was taken from his home during the Babylonian exile. He didn't complain that he was in the wrong location. Instead, he understood who he was, refusing to defile himself with the king's delicacies and wine. In return, God gave Daniel (along with three other Hebrew young men), "knowledge and skill in all literature and wisdom; and Daniel had understanding in all visions and dreams" (Daniel 1:17). In other words, Daniel chose to shine in exile.

Calendars, workout equipment, or organizational items for your home can help you begin again, but they will never be your miracle cure. David, the shepherd boy, didn't complain when he didn't have the right size armor to fight Goliath. He took a slingshot with five smooth stones and charged the Philistine, crying, "You come to me with a sword, with a spear, and with a javelin. But I come to you in the name of the Lord of hosts, the God of the armies of Israel, whom you have defied. This day the Lord will deliver you into my hand…for the battle is the Lord's, and he will give you into our hands" (1 Samuel 17:45b-47). It wasn't David's weapon that made the difference, but his faith.

Finally, being connected to the right people can certainly help, but no singular person can ultimately cause you to reach your goal. When I (Abidan) became a pastor and began my PhD work, I was working three-thousand miles away from where I grew up. I had no contacts or network to lean on. But God, in his perfect timing, began moving several key people into my life to encourage me and guide me toward achieving my goal. Even then, those connections helped me, but did not become the sole source of my achievements.

Think about Mary and Martha, two sisters who often hosted Jesus and his disciples at their home. One time, when Jesus was teaching at their home, Mary sat at his feet while Martha was busy serving others. She even complained to Jesus that Mary was not helping.

But Jesus admonished her, saying, "Martha, Martha, you are worried and troubled about many things. But one thing is needed, and Mary has chosen that good part, which will not be taken away from her" (Luke 10:41b-42). Martha was thinking if only Mary would help her, everything would be so much better. Unfortunately, she failed to realize that the goal of her existence—Jesus —was right before her eyes.

Don't get caught up in the "If-Only Syndrome." Look to God for help and not to some location, thing, or person. He will always come through for you, even if others don't.

Scriptures to Think On:

And all the children of Israel complained against Moses and Aaron, and the whole congregation said to them, "If only we had died in the land of Egypt! Or if only we had died in this wilderness! **Numbers 14:2**

Some trust in chariots, and some in horses; but we will remember the name of the Lord our God. **Psalm 20:7**

So he said, "I will do this: I will pull down my barns and build greater, and there I will store all my crops and my goods. And I will say to my soul, "Soul, you have many goods laid up for many years; take your ease; eat, drink, and be merry."' But God said to him, "Fool! This night your soul will be required of you; then whose will those things be which you have provided?' **Luke 12:18-20**

JOURNAL

_____

_____

_____

_____

_____

_____

_____

_____

_____

_____

_____

_____

_____

_____

_____

_____

27. REST

Reaching your goal requires hard work, determination, and pushing past your limits—but it also requires rest, relaxation, and recuperation. Some people are so laser-focused on achievement that they ignore the need to step back every week. Unfortunately, when those people finally arrive at the finish, they don't have the peace, joy, or satisfaction that they imagined. They overreached themselves and neglected (even mistreated) their loved ones in the process.

God's definition of rest is to cease from labor. In Genesis, he set the pattern for us: after creating the world and everything in it in six days, he rested on the seventh and even blessed and sanctified it as a Day of Rest.

Of course, God didn't need to rest. "Behold, he who keeps Israel shall neither slumber nor sleep" (Psalm 121:4). He did it to remind us that without adequate rest, we will fail to function to the level of our abilities, eventually falling apart. As the old Greco-Roman saying goes, "If you keep your bow tightly strung at all times, it will quickly break, but if you let it rest, it will be ready to use whenever you need it." True rest is complete cessation of work.

Rest is also a time to refocus your spirit on God. All

week long, you become distracted by the things of this world, the cares of this life, your worries, and pains. It's exhausting, feeling yourself getting spiritually weaker as the days drag on. Your soul needs to be recharged.

When I (Abidan) was a kid, I heard a story about a young man passing by a coal mine one Sunday morning, who inquired about several mules standing idly in a field. The old man in charge explained that the mules were used in the mines, and unless they were brought up once a week, they would go blind. So also, unless you see the Light weekly, you too will go spiritually blind. This is why weekly church attendance is imperative.

People like to say, "Oh, I worship, but I don't have to go to church. I can worship just as well on the lake, or on the golf course, or with my family at home." Sure, you can, but do you? Also, the Bible is very clear about the necessity of worshipping together in the context of the local church.

It can be very difficult to have a focused time of worship away from church. Not only that, but when you come together for worship, you are worshipping as a community. God wants you to worship him every day, six days individually and the seventh day as a community. David said in Psalm 122:1, "I was glad when they said to me, 'Let us go into the house of the Lord.'" David worshipped God individually every day, but he was filled with joy at the prospect of worshipping corporately.

Finally, times of rest are when you reconnect with the loved ones in your life, especially the young. When children are deprived of genuine, fun, and meaningful interactions with the adults in their lives, they tend to default to poor—but enticing—substitutes. If you don't take the time to reconnect with your loved ones, you'll be headed towards a "Cat's in the Cradle" relationship much worse than Harry Chapin could have ever imagined!

Take the time to experience biblical rest. It will not only recharge you and refocus your mind on God, but it will also help you finish well with the joy and satisfaction of knowing that there was no collateral damage of your loved ones in the process.

Scriptures to Think On:

Observe the Sabbath day, to keep it holy, as the Lord your God commanded you. Six days you shall labor and do all your work, but the seventh day is the Sabbath of the Lord your God. In it you shall do no work: you, nor your son, nor your daughter, nor your male servant, nor your female servant, nor your ox, nor your donkey, nor any of your cattle, nor your stranger who is within your gates, that your male servant and your female servant may rest as well as you. And remember that you were a slave in the land of Egypt, and the Lord your God brought you out from there by a mighty hand and by an outstretched arm; therefore the Lord your God commanded you to keep the Sabbath day. **Deuteronomy 5:12-15**

Every man should eat and drink and enjoy the good of all his labor—it is the gift of God. **Ecclesiastes 3:13**

Come to Me, all you who labor and are heavy laden, and I will give you rest. **Matthew 11:28**

Jesus said to his disciples, "Come aside by yourselves to a deserted place and rest a while." For there were many coming and going, and they did not even have time to eat." **Mark 6:31**

JOURNAL

_____

_____

_____

_____

_____

_____

_____

_____

_____

_____

_____

_____

28. GREATER PURPOSE

Most goals and resolutions fail to take flight because there's no weight or purpose behind them. So, you want to lose weight? That's great, but what's your ultimate goal? Do you just want to look good, feel good, and live longer? None of those goals are bad, but they're self-centered and temporal. Even if you do accomplish those goals, they won't give you the ultimate satisfaction that you were hoping for because they don't serve a greater purpose. Losing weight so you can be a healthy example for your kids, volunteer more, or help others for God's kingdom will be far more impactful and satisfying.

A wonderful example of living for the greater purpose can be found in the life of Ruth. She was a Moabite woman married to an Israelite whose family had settled in Moab due to a famine in Israel. Ten years into their marriage, Ruth's husband, brother-in-law, and father-in-law all died. Naomi (Ruth's mother-in-law) decided to go back to her homeland. She counselled her daughters-in-law to go back home and even remarry.

At first, they both insisted on going with her, but only Ruth clung to her, saying, "Entreat me not to leave you, or to turn back from following after you; For wherever you go, I will go; and wherever you lodge, I will lodge; Your people shall be my people, and your God, my God. Where you die, I will die, and there will I be buried. The Lord do so to me, and more also, if anything but death parts you and me" (Ruth 1:16-17).

Why was Ruth so insistent on following Naomi back to her ancestral home? I believe that in the ten years of being married into the family, she learned that her in-laws were God's special people carrying the hope of God's salvation for the whole world. Although this was a new beginning in her life, she wanted to remain in the line of God's Promised One.

After arriving in Bethlehem, she got Naomi's permission to glean heads of grain in the field of Boaz, a wealthy relative. When Boaz saw Ruth, she found favor in his sight, and he commanded his servants to show her extra grace. Later, she even followed the custom of the time and offered herself to Boaz as a potential bride. Long story short, Boaz was able to claim her according to the tradition of the kinsman redeemer, and they were married. As history demonstrates, Obed, their son, became the grandfather of King David.

What was Ruth's greater purpose? Be loyal to her mother-in-law? Move to a new land? Find food for her family? Get married? Have a child? Of course not! Her true purpose was to find redemption by joining the line of the coming King of Kings! Did Ruth know that she was going to be the grandmother of King David or be part of the genealogy of Jesus? Probably not, but she realized that there had to be some greater meaning beyond her immediate understanding, and she strove to live each day according to that purpose.

Examine some of the goals you have in your life. How many of them simply benefit yourself? Don't settle for those self-serving, immediate, and earthly goals. They're good to have but go deeper and find the true purpose behind those goals. God has given you unique experiences, abilities, and passions in order to use your life for his glory. Ask him to show you his greater purpose through whatever you're trying to achieve.

Keep in mind that when you begin to achieve great things for God's glory, you're signing up for the long game of life. Some of these goals may take years to accomplish, even decades. To keep from getting discouraged, choose smaller, more attainable goals that you can reach in a month's or several weeks' time. Track your progress and celebrate those little victories. That will help you keep your eyes on the big prize that God has for you!

Scriptures to Think On:

There are many plans in a man's heart, nevertheless the Lord's counsel—that will stand. **Proverbs 19:21**

Before I formed you in the womb I knew you; before you were born I sanctified you; I ordained you a prophet to the nations. **Jeremiah 1:5**

Not that I have already attained, or am already perfected; but I press on, that I may lay hold of that for which Christ Jesus has also laid hold of me. **Philippians 3:12**

[God] has saved us and called us with a holy calling, not according to our works, but according to his own purpose and grace which was given to us in Christ Jesus before time began,   **2 Timothy 1:9**

JOURNAL

_____

_____

_____

_____

_____

_____

_____

_____

_____

_____

_____

_____

_____

_____

29. DON'T LOWER THE BAR

I (Abidan) am always amused at the funny remakes of old adages, like this one: "If at first you don't succeed, try, try again." Here are just a few that have made me laugh:

"If at first you don't succeed, do it the way your wife told you!"

"If at first you don't succeed, you'll get a lot of free advice from other folks who didn't succeed either!"

"If at first you don't succeed, find out if the loser gets anything!"

"If at first you don't succeed, delegate."

"If at first you don't succeed, skydiving is not for you."

"If at first you don't succeed, lower the bar."

Unfortunately, the last one is all too true. In the face of failure, people will often lower the bar of their initial goal.

Joshua and the people of Israel won a miraculous

victory over the city of Jericho. God had commanded them to utterly destroy the city and abstain from the accursed things inside. Only the silver and gold, and vessels of bronze and iron were to be consecrated to the Lord and placed in the treasury.

Unfortunately, one man, Achan, disobeyed God and took for himself some of the forbidden items: a beautiful Babylonian garment, two hundred shekels of silver, and a wedge of gold weighing fifty shekels. Consequently, the people of Israel suffered a shameful defeat at the next battle at Ai, a much smaller city, and even lost thirty-six men.

Joshua could have lowered the bar and given up on taking Ai. Instead, he "tore his clothes, and fell to the earth on his face before the ark of the Lord until evening, he and the elders of Israel; and they put dust on their heads. And Joshua said, 'Alas, Lord GOD, why have You brought this people over the Jordan at all—to deliver us into the hand of the Amorites, to destroy us? Oh, that we had been content, and dwelt on the other side of the Jordan! O Lord, what shall I say when Israel turns its back before its enemies? For the Canaanites and all the inhabitants of the land will hear it, and surround us, and cut off our name from the earth. Then what will You do for Your great name?," (Joshua 7:6-9). God revealed to Joshua the sin of Achan. Once the accursed things and the perpetrators were destroyed, Ai became an easy victory.

Take a long, objective look at your goal. Have you lowered the bar at some point, compared to where you began? If not, great! If so, ask yourself why—could it be that there are areas in your life that need work? Is there some sin needing to be confessed? Some bad habit that needs to be discarded? Could it be that you need to devote extra time and discipline to hone some skill that God has given you to help reach your goal?

When you fail, don't lose heart. Look back to where you started to see how far you have come. But always keep your goal high because even if you don't reach the intended goal, you have still made significant strides and are further along in your journey. If you lower the bar, you'll stop prematurely. Each step of the way, look for the lessons that God wants to instill in you. Stay teachable. If you need to, take a break to regroup, then decide on your next course of action to continue working toward your goal. After all, you're only going to reach that destination by taking one step at a time.

Scriptures to Think On:

Do you see a man who excels in his work? He will stand before kings; he will not stand before unknown men. **Proverbs 22:29**

Brethren, I do not count myself to have apprehended; but one thing I do, forgetting those things which are behind and reaching forward to those things which are ahead, I press toward the goal for the prize of the upward call of God in Christ Jesus. **Philippians 3:13-14**

But you, O man of God, flee these things and pursue righteousness, godliness, faith, love, patience, gentleness. Fight the good fight of faith, **1 Timothy 6:11-12a**

JOURNAL

_____

_____

_____

_____

_____

_____

_____

_____

_____

_____

_____

_____

_____

_____

_____

_____

30. FINISH LINE

You've made it to Day Thirty, but you're not done yet! Completing this daily devotional over the past month is only the first step toward achieving your new beginning. Keep going and keep meeting and surpassing your goals every day. God has given you everything you need to begin—and finish—this new journey in your life. Continue your new habits, and don't give up!

Going forward, you'll probably have days where you may take two steps forward and one step back. Don't let yourself get discouraged. That's still progress! Remember to set small goals along the way. Always keep your eyes on Jesus, the "Author and Finisher of our faith" (Hebrews 12:2).

Even when things in life don't make sense, you can trust that God is still working. He won't stop until his work in you is complete. God is using everything in your life—good and bad—to mold you and make you into the person he created you to be. He loves you, and he won't bring you this far just to abandon you. Keep running so you can finish the race God has for you. It'll all be worth it when you hear him say, "Well done, my good and faithful servant."

We began this month by remembering Israel's failure after God commanded them to move. Instead of obeying God and moving forward, they kept circling the mountains. Keep in mind that their ultimate goal was more than just progress in general; it was to enter into the Promised Land, the prize which God had set aside for them. In fact, there were many more battles to fight in the years ahead.

In the opening of the Book of Joshua, God rouses Joshua with the words, "Moses, My servant, is dead. Now therefore, arise, go over this Jordan, you and all this people, to the land which I am giving to them— the children of Israel" (Joshua 1:2). In other words, there was no need for endlessly mourning Moses' passing and no place for sitting complacently. It was time to trust God, reject fear, and cross the Jordan River into the Promised Land.

The same truth applies to you as you reach your finish line. It's time to reject complacency and press forward toward the even bigger goals that God has for you. You never truly "arrive" in life because, ultimately, life isn't just a race with a finish line— it's also a journey with mile markers along the way. Pray and seek God's direction in what he wants you to do next. It's sad to say, but only some among the people of Israel continued to push forward. Others compromised and eventually lost God's blessings in their lives.

On Day One of this devotional, we used the illustration of being stuck in a rut. That word "rut" probably comes from the Old French word *rute* for "route." It describes the tracks left by the repeated passage of wheels over a road or path. Once the grooves got worn into the path, the wheels of passing carts would inevitably slip into the trench-like channels. Trying to climb out of those tracks can be tricky and even dangerous if the cart is particularly top-heavy. Most would decide it'd be smoother and safer to stay in the rut.

So also, in life, you will eventually find yourself in a rut. When you get so deeply stuck, it can seem impossible to get out of those well-worn trenches. It feels safer to simply stay within the familiar old tracks. You may see others attempt to climb out, but their wheels slip back in. You may have even seen some succeed, only for their ride to look bumpy and unnatural. But those bumps are a signal that they've had the courage to try something new. If your life feels too smooth, too comfortable, and too safe, it could very well be that you've fallen into another rut.

It's time to climb out.

It's time for a new beginning.

Scriptures to Think On:

So the Lord gave to Israel all the land of which he had sworn to give to their fathers, and they took possession of it and dwelt in it. The Lord gave them rest all around, according to all that he had sworn to their fathers. And not a man of all their enemies stood against them; the Lord delivered all their enemies into their hand. Not a word failed of any good thing which the Lord had spoken to the house of Israel. All came to pass. **Joshua 21:43-45**

This I recall to my mind, therefore I have hope. Through the Lord's mercies we are not consumed, because his compassions fail not. They are new every

morning; Great is Your faithfulness.
Lamentations 3:21-23

Therefore, if anyone is in Christ, he is a new creation; old things have passed away; behold, all things have become new. **2 Corinthians 5:17**

Therefore, since a promise remains of entering his rest, let us fear lest any of you seem to have come short of it. **Hebrews 4:1**

JOURNAL

_____

_____

_____

_____

_____

_____

_____

_____

_____

_____

_____

_____

_____

_____

_____

_____

_____

CONCLUSION

Every day is an opportunity for a new beginning. As Zig Ziglar would say, "Yesterday ended last night. Today is a brand-new day!" No matter who you are and where you've been, God is able and willing to help you move forward. You don't have to take this journey alone. Not only that, but he will also help you reach your destination.

If you're still feeling unable to begin, ask yourself these questions:

- What is keeping me from stepping out of the rut?
- Can I see that I am stuck in a rut?
- Why am I afraid to step forward?
- Can I see the presence of God with me?
- Can I see the possibilities that God has for me?
- How will I impact the world by making the new beginning?

Remember the final words of Jesus to his disciples "lo, I am with you always, even to the end of the age" (Matthew 28:20).

ABOUT THE AUTHORS

Abidan Shah (PhD, Southeastern Baptist Theological Seminary) is the lead pastor of Clearview Church in Henderson, NC and professor of New Testament and Greek. He also serves as a chaplain to the local hospital, police department, and fire department. His other works include *30 Days Through a Crisis* and *Changing the Goalpost of New Testament Textual Criticism*. For more information, visit abidanshah.com.

Nicole Shah (BA in Christian Counseling, pursuing a Masters Degree in Marriage and Family Therapy at Toccoa Falls College) is active in ministry alongside her husband. Nicole also co-authored *30 Days Through a Crisis*. The Shahs have four children and have been in ministry for 25 years. For more information, visit clearviewbc.org.

ENJOY MORE GREAT TITLES FROM
ABIDAN AND NICOLE SHAH!

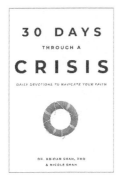

What will people say about you when the crisis is over? Written in response to the pandemic, this 30-day devotional by Abidan and Nicole Shah will help you navigate any crisis you may be facing.

Available in paperback, e-book, and audiobook formats!

Many scholars argue that the original text of Scripture is lost and unable to be recovered. In Dr. Shah's dissertation, he traces this question through the years as the field of textual criticism has shifted and changed. Learn to understand critical issues related to the text of Scripture and solidify your confidence in the Word of God!

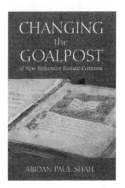

Want to liven up your commute? Tune in today!

Available on The Truth App, iHeartradio, and your favorite podcasting platform!

Made in the USA
Columbia, SC
23 December 2022

74927268R00083